HAPPILY EVER NOW

HAPPILY EVER NOW

Discover Your Self Worth

Wendy D Bowen

BALBOA
PRESS
A DIVISION OF HAY HOUSE

Balboa Press books may be ordered through booksellers or by contacting:

Balboa Press
A Division of Hay House
1663 Liberty Drive
Bloomington, IN 47403
www.balboapress.com
1-(877) 407-4847

Because of the dynamic nature of the Internet, any web addresses or links contained in this book may have changed since publication and may no longer be valid. The views expressed in this work are solely those of the author and do not necessarily reflect the views of the publisher, and the publisher hereby disclaims any responsibility for them.

The author of this book does not dispense medical advice or prescribe the use of any technique as a form of treatment for physical, emotional, or medical problems without the advice of a physician, either directly or indirectly. The intent of the author is only to offer information of a general nature to help you in your quest for emotional and spiritual well-being. In the event you use any of the information in this book for yourself, which is your constitutional right, the author and the publisher assume no responsibility for your actions.

Any people depicted in stock imagery provided by Thinkstock are models, and such images are being used for illustrative purposes only. Certain stock imagery © Thinkstock.

Printed in the United States of America

ISBN: 978-1-4525-6732-7 (sc)
ISBN: 978-1-4525-6733-4 (e)
ISBN: 978-1-4525-6734-1 (hc)
Library of Congress Control Number: 2013901099
Balboa Press rev. date: 3/13/2013

CONTENTS

Foreword ix

Preface xiii

Acknowledgements xvii

Introduction xix

Our Own Journey xxiii

'Part I: Awakening 1

    Chapter 1: The Desire for Acceptance 3

    Chapter 2: Discovery of the Ego 5

    Chapter 3: The Princess at the Ball—the Need to Be
        Special 11

    Chapter 4: The Desire to Be Perfect 15

    Chapter 5: The Fear of Loss and Being Alone 19

    Chapter 6: Know Thyself 23

    Chapter 7: Giving Away Your Power 35

    Chapter 8: Living without Regrets 39

    Chapter 9: The End of the Fairy Tale 43

    Chapter 10: The Princess Tries to Rescue Herself—
        Independence 47

Chapter 11: Prince Charming—Feeling Loved and
    Safe 49

Chapter 12: Surviving Turmoil and Change 55

Chapter 13: Love Validated—the Doghouse Theory ... 65

Chapter 14: Constant Transformation 67

Part II: Climbing out of the Potholes 71

Chapter 15: Forgiveness Is the Key 73

Chapter 16: Be Flexible 75

Chapter 17: Allowing 79

Chapter 18: The Universal Kick in the Butt—
    Accepting Change 83

Chapter 19: Your Inner Voice—Finding It and
    Listening to It 87

Chapter 20: Loving Beyond the Ego 91

Chapter 21: Outgrow Your Problems 97

Chapter 22: Escape from the Dungeon—Taking
    Responsibility for Your Life 101

Part III: Avoiding the Potholes 105

Chapter 23: Mirror, Mirror 107

Chapter 24: Humility 111

Chapter 25: Vulnerability 113

Chapter 26: Knowing What You Really Want 117

Chapter 27: The Princess at the Ball—Every
    Relationship Is Special 121

Chapter 28: Self-Love 125

Chapter 29: Spiritual Practice 131

Chapter 30: Be of Service 133

Chapter 31: Happily Ever Now—a Promise to
    Myself..137

Chapter 32: Loving with Awareness............................141

Chapter 33: My Interior Castle........................145

Part VI: Happily Ever Now 149

Chapter 34: Enjoy the Journey 151

Chapter 35: New Love.................................... 155

Appendix 1 157

Appendix 2 : Getting out of the Potholes (Getting
    Unstuck) 159

Appendix 3: Filling the Potholes 161

Further Notes and References 163

Foreword

Congratulations! You have chosen to read a very important book. There are many reasons for something to have importance. It may be something that acts as a catalyst to view a relationship differently, or, helps us obtain a goal or a skill. It may be something that helps us view ourselves differently or to solve a challenge or problem. To me, the most profound reason for something to have importance is that it encourages me to view myself, others and the world through a different lens and this change has an element of permanence to it in that I cannot return to the "way it was before".

A very wise teacher and colleague of mine once shared with me, "Experiences without reflection are meaningless. It is reflection that creates growth." I have never forgotten this and have applied this to my work as a teacher and my relationships. Sometimes this has been challenging because reflection can open up a Pandora of insights that perhaps may be unsettling. Often, though, this is exactly what is needed to move forward and grow. This book embodies this ideal regarding reflection and growth. Through this book of reflection and the parallel story of the princess and the prince I have been encouraged, as the reader, to reflect upon my life, events, relationships, perceptions, interpretations and roles. This book has encouraged me to grow in a new and unexpected direction and to take a fresh look at the social norms within which I live. It has also encouraged me to ask myself some insightful questions and importantly, to seek answers to those questions through reflection. My hope is that you too will experience an equally positive effect in your life through reading this book and sharing in Wendy's experiences and journey.

As Albert Schweitzer has stated,

"If mankind is not to perish after all the dreadful things it has done and gone through, then a new spirit must emerge. And this new spirit is coming not with a roar but with a quiet birth, not with grand measure and words but with an imperceptible change in the atmosphere – a change in which each of us is participating..."[1]

quoted by Robert Holden in Success Intelligence

This book embodies one woman's journey to this place of rebirth. It has been a long and sometimes arduous road filled with many, many opportunities for growth, reflection and self-discovery. Wendy's ability to write with honesty and clarity about her experiences enables the reader, to connect to her and even more importantly, to ourselves. From the time we were very young, I have had the deep realization that Wendy was on a quest. As a child, I was unsure of what the purpose of this quest was however I have always had an understanding of its importance. Wendy consistently, as a child, broke free from the norms of society. Most distinctly are memories of her practicing and playing hockey before girls' hockey was commonly accepted. I recall early morning practices at the local arena where she would arrive fully dressed so she would not have to deal with locker room issues. I recall many in the stands, where I waited patiently with my nose in my most recent favourite book, marvelling at her skill and talent on the ice not knowing that she was a girl. I recall her challenging the educational norms of boys participating in shop class and girls participating in home economics class. I recall her in elementary school, thinking it was grossly unfair that her friend Anthony should have to sit in hall all by himself during the Lord's Prayer and having the insight, compassion and fortitude at such a young age to insist on sitting with him so that he wouldn't feel alone. In her many relationships over the years I have witnessed Wendy deal with hurt, thoughtlessness and pain with kindness and love. Wendy has always demonstrated a strong belief in the goodness of others even when this has resulted in amplifying her own sense of hurt or pain. Wendy's quest, I now realize as an adult, has been to love herself as deeply as she has always loved others. She is the glue that binds, even if she hasn't always known this. She connects people to each other by connecting with them herself. Her ability to do this effectively has only strengthened over the years has she has become more aware of her own self and grown in self- love through her journey of reflection.

As Wendy quoted from Carylyn Myss

"It is though the understanding of ourselves that we are better able to be authentic in our relationships with others. Such understanding requires work to move beyond the mind and emotions to the interior wall of the soul."[2]

I would venture to add to this that the key to this process is reflection and a willingness to acknowledge and embrace who you are. This book is one person's journey to do just that and this is why I believe this is a very important book.

May you be blessed on your journey of self - discovery.

Cheryl Franklin

PREFACE

Happily Ever Now?

*History has a way of repeating itself
until the lesson is learned*

The universe will offer us the experiences that we need in order to learn what we need to learn. The universe will bring other people into our lives to help us with our learning and growth.

What were the lessons that I needed to learn before I would meet my prince and live happily ever after? That is how it is supposed to be, is it not?

One day, while journaling, I started to wonder why it bothered me so much that I did not have someone in my life wanting to marry me. There was nobody who loved me enough to say, "I would love to be with you for the rest of my life. Will you marry me?"

This book is the answer to my question (why did I want someone to ask me to marry him). What did I feel that I was missing in my life if I was not married? What did I think about myself? What was I doing in my relationships? The answers to some of our greatest questions are answered through our experiences.

This book is not just for the single person who is searching for love, a soul mate, a lifetime partner. This book is one person's journey—my journey—but it is a journey that we all take towards discovering our true or authentic selves. It is our relationships with other people that are the essence of the journey—whether you are in a marriage, a partnership, or a close friendship.

In *Happily Ever Now,* I explore (through my past and present relationships) some of the pitfalls or potholes we tend to encounter during our journey. I also explore some of the ways in which we get out of the holes we fall into. Plus, I examine how we can make changes in our choices and behaviours in order to avoid falling into these traps.

This book is my *symbolic sight journey* (an idea derived from Caroline Myss's *Sacred Contracts*)[1] into my own purpose, value, and worth. It is about my own growth and development. It is about my relationships with others and this universe. It has been said that our relationships are really just mirrors that reflect back to us the things that we ourselves need to work on. When someone does something that bothers us, we can learn something about ourselves through that experience. This can only happen if we are actually paying attention to what we are doing. *Living with awareness* is the phrase that continues to show up in my life. As my good friend Brianne said once (a few times actually), "Awareness sucks."

After much review and consideration, we decided that awareness is the sunlight that melts our unconscious, programmed beliefs. Without awareness, we keep doing the same things over and over again. When we do this and expect different results, we are acting insane (reportedly according to Einstein). How can we change what we are doing if we are not aware of what we are doing?

When another person holds up a mirror—you typically know this is happening when you are annoyed by what the other person is saying or asking—you can choose to look deeply into your own soul and discover what it is about the situation that you find frustrating or annoying. You can use that situation to learn about yourself. Or you can choose to shut your eyes and go back to sleep. You can hope that, when you wake up, the truth will no longer be there, staring back at you. You can choose to live in a dream state (or *illusion,* as it is often called).

It is not easy work to reflect on our behaviours and actions and get beyond the illusion to the truth. The truth about who we truly are has quite often been hidden by layers of other people's expectations, beliefs, desires, and dreams. It is often easier to lie in a deep sleep and dream. It feels safe to sleep … and it's more peaceful. Why would someone choose to wake up and walk the path of awareness? It is my opinion that, if we are to *truly* live a life of purpose and achieve our highest and best potential and truly be of service, we need to be awake.

When we sleepwalk through life, there is more potential to fall into the holes or traps that are set out. For some reason, this makes me think of when Winnie the Pooh set out to trap the Heffalump and ended up falling into his own trap (because the bait he set was honey).[2] We all know that Pooh loves honey. He had wanted the honey so badly that he forgot it was part of his own trap.

How many times do you want to repeat the same lesson? How many holes or traps do you want to fall into and try to get out of?

People talk about living happily ever after. After what? After we get all the money we desire? After we find our one true lifetime love or perfect partner? After we have our house, two and a half kids, and dog? After we have established our careers to the point that we don't have to think about our jobs?

I was told once that I spend too much time in the past or in the future. At times, someone else's honest opinion can hurt us—but it can also elevate us. It can force us to go inside of ourselves and reflect on our own opinions and what we perceive to be the truth. When my friend made that comment, I reflected on those words.

Now is the only time that we truly have.

According to Don Miguel Ruiz,[3] you should not believe

anything that you read in this book or any book. You should question and doubt everything. What is contained in this book is just my opinion, the way that I am making sense of my life's journey. It is not your life you are going to read about.

Why write a book, then, if it may not be true. Because it is my truth as I know it and observe it. I have read many books about other people's truths and life perspectives that have given me insight and inspiration. I have taken the information that others have provided through their stories and reflected on my own feelings and life events. Perhaps what you read here will be that for you: a source of inspiration, hope, and reflection. Perhaps, through my story, you will be able to discover that you are not alone on the path to discovering your purpose and worthiness.

Acknowledgements

There are several very important individuals who have contributed to my personal growth and development. First and foremost, I must acknowledge my parents. They have provided me with a stable home environment, which helped me develop a solid foundation. They have continued to be there through my life's journey, listening to me as I sort things out. They never tell me what I need to do, and they always offer me unconditional love and support. I must also thank my sister. She has been with me throughout the whole journey. I am grateful for my sister and love her very much. Although we had our share of differences in our early years, she has offered me insight and gentle guidance. She never tells me what I should do; rather, she makes suggestions. This may be one of the great qualities that she picked up from our mom. I never have felt judged by my family.

I cannot forget about my brother who has challenged me to give without expectations and love unconditionally. Though my relationship with my brother is somewhat estranged, it is said that those who challenge us in life are our teachers. Verse twenty-seven in the Tao discusses what I think my brother represents in my life: "What is a good man but a bad man's teacher, what is a bad man but a good man's job."[1]

And then there are the relationships I have had with people outside of my family unit. I want to thank all those people who I have considered friends and partners along the way. When we start these friendships, we think that they will last a lifetime. What lasts a lifetime are the psychological imprints of these people on us. Sometimes this is good; sometimes this is not so good. I believe that part of the challenge when a relationship ends is taking the good and leaving the not so good (after having learned from it). The endings were a source of sadness and emotional pain, but there was never any bitterness. These friendships and relationships helped me become stronger in my personal connections. It was often dealing with the loss of the friendship or relationship (either through personal growth or physical distance) that helped develop my third chakra (personal power).

I will refer to the chakras occasionally throughout this book. These are well defined in Caroline Myss's book, *Anatomy of the Spirit.*[2] These are basically the energy systems of our beings, and they are related to different aspects of our life. For example, the first chakra is called the root chakra, and it is related to the familial or tribal energy connections in our life.

Of these friends and partners, there are a few who continue to hold a special place in my heart and in my soul. These are the relationships through which I have done the greatest learning and growth. It is a love that everyone should hope to experience at some time in their lives. Of all these people, my dear friend and soul companion, Brianne (with her insights and intuition), has helped me most to understand the matters of the heart. She guided me towards understanding past relationships and myself. It was her intuition into my emotional self that forced me to answer some challenging questions that I perhaps never would have otherwise asked. She helped open up my heart so I was able to receive great love. She challenged me to discover my own self-worth. Brianne is a gifted, talented, and strong woman, and I am truly grateful for her existence in my life. She helped transform my life from reading about knowledge to putting it into practice. She has been one of my greatest teachers to date. The greatest lesson that I have learned so far is that it is impossible to receive great love if you do not feel worthy of it.

All the people who have come into my life or left my life, I consider you all kindred spirits and guides of my life journey. Thank you all for your love, support, and guidance along the way.

INTRODUCTION

Once upon a time, in a land not so far, far away, lived a beautiful princess. At one time, she might have known she was a beautiful princess. She did not know it now, though, because there was a spell that had been cast upon her that made her unaware she was a princess at all. It was a dark shadow that blanketed the light within her, not allowing her to see her true beauty.

The spell had caused the beautiful princess to seek validation of her worth and beauty outside of herself. She discovered at an early age that she was able to gain the attention and approval of others if she did what they expected of her (or what she thought they expected). Feelings of acceptance and love resulted, and the value of pleasing others was reinforced. Pleasing others to gain their love, approval, and acceptance, however, came at a very high cost. That was part of the curse.

The beautiful princess met a few princes along the road that she travelled. One day, she met a prince with whom she fell madly in love. He was charming, romantic, and kind. The princess had always dreamed of getting married. Despite her deep love for this prince, it was not the happily ever after fairy tale romance. The prince chose another, and the beautiful princess's heart was shattered into several pieces. The princess felt betrayed, abandoned, unworthy, and alone. There was a huge hole, and she was filled with emptiness. Unable to fully trust her heart again, she locked it up in the dungeon (where she thought it would be safe).

In order to fill the hole inside of herself—where her heart

had once beat so strongly—the princess busied herself with a career of serving others. It was easier to take care of other people's problems than to look at her own. She was still under the spell.

The princess left her homeland and travelled far, far away. She tried to forget the past and the pain, but it clung to her. No matter how far she travelled, the blackness of the pain followed her like a shadow in the night. It was her fear that allowed it to follow her. The princess did not realize her fear, so she did not turn to face it. She just got busier.

The beautiful princess was able to find a sense of safety and comfort through the company of a wonderful companion. Together, they travelled and explored a faraway land. The memory of her prince and the desire to have a meaningful relationship, however, still haunted the princess. The beautiful princess still wanted to find true and lasting love. She still dreamed of finding another prince and getting married. Love—unconditional, fully accepting, and committed love—eluded her ... or perhaps she eluded it out of fear. Afraid to open her heart to another for fear of the pain of a broken heart, she avoided true intimacy (which involves being vulnerable). She was afraid to unlock her caged heart because she didn't want it to be shattered again. The princess had promised her heart that she would protect it from further harm. Keeping her promises was a strength of the princess (sometimes to a fault).

One day, the princess met a spirit guide who told the princess that she had angels around her. She saw the princess's heart locked tightly in the cage. Only the key of forgiveness would unlock the princess's heart and allow her to fully receive love again. Forgiveness of herself and forgiveness of those whom she had felt hurt by was the key to her healing.

One day, on the majestic ocean, the beautiful princess met a beautiful kindred spirit disguised as someone in need of her help. Because the princess liked to help other people in order to avoid worrying about herself, she was lured into rescuing the kindred spirit. The kindred spirit held up the magic mirror for the beautiful princess. The magic mirror allowed the princess to look at herself and see her own reflection. The magic mirror allowed her to see past the ego's spell that had covered her true beauty and inner light with a dark blanket. The magic mirror reflected the beautiful princess's own inner light, self-worth, and love. The magic mirror allowed her to discover her true self.

This is a story about discovering your own inner beauty, loving yourself, learning to let go of fear and desire, finding inner peace and joy, and living *happily ever now*. There is quite often a mismatch between what we show outwardly to others and what we are truly feeling inside.

Our Own Journey

We all have our own path or journey. The analogy of our life journey being like travelling across the country in a car can be quite powerful.

I like to know where I am going, to plan my trips. You can drive across the country without a final destination, but how will you know when you have arrived? You might be alone on the trip or have a passenger. Your car might be filled with a family. Perhaps your car has all your friends in it (even in the back hatch, which has happened on occasion). Your journey might have all of these varied situations at different times in your life.

There were times when I felt alone on my journey because there was no one in my passenger seat who was a fully committed partner (which, to me, means a connected mind, body, and soul). Have you ever noticed, though, that when you are driving by yourself, you can experience times of great reflection and growth? When I travel by myself, I listen to Hay House radio[1] or Hay House authors such as Cheryl Richardson, Wayne Dyer, and Robert Holden (a few of my favorites). I listen, reflect, learn, and grow.

It used to be that I always wanted someone to be with me, right beside me. What I have recently discovered, however, is that I enjoy my alone travel time. Recently, I went on a trip to San Diego by myself. There, I went to a Hay House writers and presenters workshop. This was a huge step for me. I met several wonderful people there, with two of whom I really connected. In our brief weekend together, they touched my life tremendously. Fiona Fay from Ireland (author of *Who Is God?*

You Are[2] and, Sam Lamont from my hometown: Peterborough, Ontario. As I write this, I am awaiting my trip to New York City for the Robert Holden coaching success intelligence course. I was initially really nervous about going on my own, but I have since become more excited about going and the possibilities of who I might meet on the trip. I know that, when I travel with a friend or go to courses with friends, I do not venture out on my own to meet people.

It was when I started to have real faith and develop a belief in the higher power we call God (and work on my spiritual self on a consistent basis) that I felt less alone. It is like the poem "Footprints" says: "My precious, precious child, I love you and would never leave you. During your times of trial and suffering, when you saw only one set of footprints, it was I that carried you."[3]

One of my greatest insights to date has been that I don't always get to know why things happen. My desire to logically explain everything that happens is very strong. In my mind, I have a destination, but life sometimes has a different route for me. Why? I can only go to the grace of faith and trust that the universe has my best intentions in mind. As I travel, I can only see so far down the road—and how far depends on the conditions around me. Is it night or day? Is it foggy or raining? Is the moon shining light through the night? There have been obstacles that I have had to drive around and detours that I was not expecting to take. The detours, often, are a source of frustration at the time because I just want to get on with the journey and arrive at my destination.

**"The purpose of life is not to arrive
safely at our destination."**[4]

- Robert Holden

What if this detour is showing us a better way? Helping us avoid a pothole? Taking us to magnificent places that we would not have otherwise seen?

Are you driving your own car, or are you going where someone else wants you to go? This was my challenge in my relationships. Not knowing who I truly was or focusing on my own journey, I would adjust my route to fit into someone else's trip. Sometimes we travel alone, sometimes with others. Our relationships (passengers) support us on our journey. These people hopefully guide us along the roads of life without telling us which way we should go and without putting up roadblocks or barriers. I want to help people reach their destinations, their highest and best potential. I want to help people overcome barriers and obstacles.

"Live full, die empty."[5]

- Les Brown

When we get to the end of our journey here on earth, let the gas tank be empty.

The journey of discovering your authentic self is not without potholes. Brianne would tell you that it seems like I hit every pothole on the road when she is driving with me. It is like I try to hit them. I have had some emotional potholes in my life as well. With each hole, however, I evolve.

At times, we can feel lost while on the journey. There is nothing worse than when I am going to an unfamiliar destination and feel like I am lost. It is frightening. Even the thought of going somewhere new is anxiety inducing. It is unknown and unfamiliar. What is up ahead? Will I be safe? As I mentioned earlier, I like to plan. I want to know when everything is happening—what time things leave or arrive. I want to be there ahead of time (last minute is awful for me because I don't want to miss the boat … or plane). I will use Google Maps for the route and commit much of it to memory. I will have an idea of certain landmarks that I should be seeing to know that I am on track. The thought of travelling without a plan is terrifying for me.

It is this planning and desire to stay safe that has kept

me from travelling to certain places on my own. It is this same need to know that I will be safe that has kept me from venturing into many (possibly) good relationships. I wanted to know that it would be forever before I opened up my heart and showed vulnerability. We are motivated by two things in life: avoidance of pain and attainment of pleasure. Will we let fear of pain and pain avoidance rob us of the potential joy that life has in store for us?

During my journey, I have come across a couple of affirmations that have really helped me:

The universe is conspiring in my favor.

I deserve only the best.

Do I expect to get to a point in my life that there are no potholes? If my road is loaded with potholes and I am finding the travel frustrating, then yes, perhaps I need to re-examine my road map and see whether there is a different way with fewer potholes. Perhaps the different road is just about staying true to my self. As one of my clients said, "[You should] not abandon your self" in order to be with another person. Life is about maintaining our identity while travelling with someone else. I need to know who I am in order to do this.

It is my hope that, by reading this book, you will be able to take the time to start your journey into discovering your own self-worth. I hope you will discover a way to fill in the potholes in your life (or avoid some of them) to make the trip smoother and more blissful.

'Part I:
Awakening

There was no big event that led to my awakening. I would have never made it onto *Oprah* if the show was still on the air. Prince Charming did not come along, kiss me, rouse me from my slumber, and escort me to live happily ever after. Unless, of course you consider, Wayne Dyer to be my knight in shining armor.

Personal growth and inspirational/motivational books have been a part of my life since my early twenties. I was accumulating a lot of great knowledge, but was I taking the steps to practice what I was putting into my head? Not consistently. Typical of many of us, I would wake up a little bit, roll over, and fall back to sleep. I would wake up again—perhaps a bit more alert—and hit the snooze button again. This makes me think of when Brianne tells me that she isn't ready to work on that part of being awake yet, that she is going to leave it for next year. This always makes me laugh because, unlike most of us who don't realize that we are falling back asleep, she is aware that she wants to leave that work until later. She is more aware than I think I could even dream of being.

One Christmas, I went to the west coast of Vancouver Island (Tofino) for the week with my good friend. It was a time to recharge the battery. My father told me that I needed to "get a life" because all I was focused on was my career (work and education). It was true. Keeping busy is a great way to avoid reflection. The book *Wisdom of the Ages* by Dr. Wayne Dyer[1] decided to make the trip with me (books choose me). The book hit me upside the head, and I realized just how out of balance I was. My table was tipped—I was not paying attention to my spiritual side at all. I made a promise to myself (I am very good at keeping my promises) that I would do something every day (read or journal, for example) that would focus on my spiritual or soul self. That was my shift, and it just continues to expand my horizons. I have remained awake since that time in Tofino.

There was no big fall from grace before I started to make changes in my life. I guess I do try to practice what I preach (as a physiotherapist) in terms of prevention. When we need to make changes in our lives but don't listen, the universe just keeps turning up the volume until we start listening. If we choose to stop and listen, we will hear what we are being guided to do.

Chapter 1:
The Desire for Acceptance

Have you ever felt like you were alone when you were surrounded by a group of people? Have you ever felt like you were not good enough? Have you ever felt like you don't really fit in? Have you been waiting to meet the person of your dreams, the perfect partner who would make you feel like you were perfect, give you the perfect life, and make your life feel complete? Most people who know me would be totally shocked to discover that I have felt this way (and still do at times).

Growing up as a tomboy, I always felt a bit different. I was not a girly-girl as my niece once pointed out. My preference was to play football, hockey, and other sports with the boys rather than skipping and hopscotch with the girls. Dresses were absent from my wardrobe; they were replaced with pants, T-shirts, and runners. My hair was short and dark, as was my skin. Looking like a little boy worked to my advantage at times, like when my dad registered me for power skating (only for boys) when I was just six years old. He used my middle name, Dale. The story of me getting hit in the head with a baseball bat (I struck the boy out, and it upset him, I guess) is a telling one. I walked home with blood coming out of my head, and a neighborhood girl screamed, "There is a little Chinese boy bleeding to death." That story always gets a few laughs. My father was shocked to see his little white girl with blood gushing from her forehead. Yes, being a tomboy sometimes worked to my advantage.

3

Being a girl, at times, had its disadvantages. Having to do home economics (cooking and sewing) instead of shop class seemed unfair to me. There was also the time that I tried to go back into class after recess through the boy's entrance because I wanted to hang out with my friends longer (they were all boys). I was told I could not. Yes, I know that I still need to forgive this teacher. It must have had a huge impact on me at the time, though, because I can still recall who the teacher was.

Looking like a little boy but being a girl also had its disadvantages in the area of self-esteem. Just like everyone else, though, I just wanted to fit in. I wanted to be accepted for who I was, even if I was not like everyone else.

Self-acceptance seems to be one of the greatest challenges that we all face. Do you feel accepted for who you really feel you are, or do you like me and so many others who wear masks when they go out to the ball? We want to belong, so we do what is needed to fit in. But what do we give up, and how do we betray ourselves when we try to fit in?

Chapter 2:
Discovery of the Ego

What is our ego? We are led to believe that the ego is not a good thing. But why would we all have one if it did not serve a purpose? This was a great debate that Brianne and I had. I kept wanting to find a purpose for my ego. I felt that it was my ego that motivated me to do the best that I could. It was my ego that wanted me to be the best physiotherapist in order to help people. It was the ego that dragged one of my clients out of bed each morning to get her ready for the day (despite the fact that she was depressed about a relationship). She did not want her ex to see her distraught. She wanted to look prettier than the other woman. Of course, it was my ego that was trying to convince me and everyone around me that it has a purpose. It wanted to survive. My ego did motivate me to strive to be the best, but out of wanting to be recognized as the best. As I had this aha moment, I thought *That little bugger is sneaky and clever.*

Many of the inspirational leaders suggest that we need to live ego-free. I was reading an article in a health magazine about ego versus self. It talked about the ego being our primary defense or self-protection mechanism. In a survival of the fittest kind of life, we do need our ego ready and available. This is the illusion of separation—right from a single cell (which has the primary goal of survival) up through the multi-cellular organisms (animals and humans). An animal's instinct is to survive. Single cells come together to form a community in order to increase their chance of survival. Human beings can also form communities in order to increase their chance of survival. As we come together—and in order to survive—we have to start doing things that consider the whole organism or community. We join with others to increase our chance of survival. The ego, however, would have us believe that we need to be separate in order to survive, not working as a community. Is marriage a way of forming that community? Does marriage end the separation?

"Whom God has joined as one, the ego cannot put asunder."[1]

- A Course in Miracles

What happens when a single cell in the body starts to put itself first, ahead of the needs of the whole body? It is called cancer. The cells start to attack and kill the host, which it actually relies upon for its own survival.

What happens to us as humans when we let our ego demands get ahead of us and don't stop to consider how they affect the other person or the whole community? We get negative interactions. This is not to say that each individual cell or person should not be taking care of primary needs first. Just like when we are flying on an airplane and we are told to put on our own oxygen masks first, (before attending to the needs of others), we need to do this for our own physical, emotional, intellectual, spiritual health as well. If you pass out from exhaustion, you can't do your part in supporting the community. We are interdependent, so we rely on one another.

What is in the one is in the whole; what affects one affects the whole. The ego represents the *me,* not the *we.*

In *A Course in Miracles,* there is information on different kinds of love. The ego love is inconsistent, and it is dependent upon what the other person is able to do or not do for us. The ego love would have the other person fill our voids. My own fears of being lonely or my need of outside confirmation of my self-worth or beauty were a couple of my own voids that I sought to have filled by the other significant person in my life.

This is not to say that I did not feel a deeper level of love for these people in my life. I have felt the soul level of love, which is more consistent. It is the love that is always there regardless of what the other person is doing for us. This is the love that, for me, stays—even when the relationship changes.

And then there is the God level of love. God loves everyone all the time. God only wants the best for us, but God allows us the freedom of choice. This level of love is without judgment. This level of love is totally accepting. This level of love is inclusive, not exclusive.

If you are feeling disappointment, bitterness, anger, or resentment when a relationship ends, a good question to ask is, on what level did I love this person? Ego-based love is conditional. Robert Holden said it best when he stated that we cannot get hurt in a relationship if we were not expecting something from the other person.[2]

When I examine past relationships, I do see all levels of love. I said once that I have never fallen out of love. Falling in love with someone has always been a beautiful and magical experience for me. I do believe that all of my greatest and truest loves have been at the level of soul love. That is the love that has lingered. Was there ego love that entered the relationship? Without a doubt there was. Typically, this seemed to rear its head once there was a more physical intimacy that evolved.

A Course in Miracles says the following:

"The body is the ego's chosen weapon for seeking power through relationships."

All of a sudden, feelings of jealousy would emerge where there did not seem to be any before. Jealousy would arise if the other person was not spending enough time with me (ego's expectation and desire). The ego would tell me that I should be worried because, if they were not making the time for me, it might mean they did not love me as much anymore. My ego would feel threatened. Perhaps I was not good enough. It would have to compete for the other person's love, attention, and affection.

The only way that the ego was allowed to enter into what started as a loving relationship from the soul level was my own feelings of inadequacy; my own feelings of not being good enough or worthy of the other person's love; my own doubts and lack of self-love.

Once upon a time, there was no ego …

What would life be like without the ego? If you really want to know, just watch a newborn baby or young child. They live in the now. They do not judge. They are filled with joy. Just listen to the child's laughter.

Most of us will not be able to remember the time before our ego started to develop because it was likely before the age of five. Wayne Dyer told a story about a young boy talking with his new baby brother and asking the new baby to remind him what it was like to be close to God because he thought he was starting to forget. It is true that we are most like God when we are younger.[3]

Jill Bolte Taylor, author of *My Stroke of Insight* [4] describes it as a state of bliss. The left hemisphere of her brain shut down after a stroke. The left brain is the analytical brain. It is the brain of the "world of the ten thousand things," as the Tao says.[5] This description is so fitting because it often feels like I have ten thousand things to do every day and no time to do them all. It is our world of form—who we are in this world. This part of my brain tells me my name is Wendy, that I am female, that I work as a physiotherapist, that my parents' names are Harold and Janice Bowen, that I have an older sister and younger brother. This part of my brain tells me where I live. Without that part of her brain, Jill said she did not know all of those things. But what she was able to do was pick up on the energy. She was energy. She could sense if the energy from someone was positive or negative. When we move beyond the ego brain into our God brain, it is joyous and full of bliss.

Can we get back to this state of being while still living in this world of ten thousand things? Yes, we can. Can we have a love with another person that does not involve the ego? I believe we can, although this is something that I am still working on. I believe that anything is possible. Getting there does involve being awake and aware of what is driving our behaviours and our decisions.

CHAPTER 3:
THE PRINCESS AT THE BALL—
THE NEED TO BE SPECIAL

Oh the thought of puppy love. I can go right back to how it felt when I was kissed for the first time. Okay, so I don't really remember the feeling of being kissed, I just remember wanting to punch the guy for telling me I had a mustache. Talk about a blow to my ego and my self-esteem. It was grade five. That was when I first started to become interested in boys (besides playing with them on the football field). It was the time of passing notes back and forth in class asking, "Do you want to go out with me? Check yes or no."

I don't think I even knew what *going out* meant at the time. The only thing I knew was that it was nice to have someone interested in going out with you. It made me feel special. This was not the start of the ego needing external validation, but it was the first time I recall wanting that one special person to pay attention to just me. I guess that is what going out is all about. Prior to that time, I was just friends with everyone. I don't even recall feeling that I had a best friend prior to that time—it felt like everyone was the same.

This is the lesson from the Tao's twentieth verse:[1] we are all one, originating from the same source. Somewhere along our path, however, we forget this and start to see differences in people. It is the true master who does not notice that he is different than others.[2]

Our second chakra deals with one-to-one relationships with others (outside of our family). It deals with sexual energy, power, and money. The negative side to this chakra arises when we try to control others or allow ourselves to be controlled by others in our relationships. Allowing this to happen causes a loss of energy from this chakra.[3]

It wasn't until about grade five or six that I started to have more special friendships with my female peers. Still, I don't recall ever having a best friend until I was in high school. There was a group of four females with whom I hung around in grades seven and eight, but we were never best friends with only one person. Prior to that time, most of my friends were boys.

I don't think I really had a boyfriend until grade seven. He was one year ahead of me. I know we dated for most of that year, and we broke it off when he was heading to another school (high school). I did not think it was fair to him to try to have a relationship with me when he was moving into the next part of his life. I can't believe I was mature enough to think that way back then. I knew it was the right choice when he met up with another girl and they became a hot item at the high school. It was still a bit of a blow that I was right, however.

John was the guy I was interested in dating when I was in grade eight. What it was about him, I can't recall, other than the fact that I thought he was cute. I was supposed to go to my graduation dance with him, and I was so excited. This was the reason why I was so devastated when I found out (not by him, through another friend) that John was no longer going to go to the dance. This was my first experience with rejection that caused me to cry. I was devastated. What was wrong with me that he did not want to take me? For the record, he did not take anyone else to the dance—he just did not want to go. But I took it personally.

Now it was between a couple of my other male friends—who was going to take me to the dance? Neither of them said they wanted to take me; instead, they said the other person could take me. That did not make me feel special. Again, I felt rejected because neither one said, "I really want to take you." This was "giving away my power," Brianne would tell me now. Giving away my power entailed letting someone else's actions (or lack of action) dictate how worthy I felt about myself. Watch out for this pothole. It is a big one. I ended up going with the guy I dated through my first few years of high school.

CHAPTER 4:
THE DESIRE TO BE PERFECT

The Perfectionist

Today I read about
the perfectionist …
whose greatest fear
is failure.
For failure is weakness
and he would not like to look weak
in front of you.
So now
The perfectionist
Himself cannot achieve personal greatness
for he sets his goals low
and hides from opportunity.
He has no enemies
but himself.
One mistake and he feels
worthless.
There is no place for mistakes.

Today I read about
the perfectionist.
Memories of childhood and yesterday viewed.
I realize her words were true.
I wasn't reading a book;
I was looking in the mirror.

So many of us strive to be perfect. But why? For me it is a way of getting the love that I so desperately want. If I am perfect in the eyes of another person—especially the person I love dearly—that person will want to be with me. It is my ego that tells me that I need to be perfect in order to be worthy of another person's love. If I am not perfect, I experience guilt.

My mother recognized this quality of perfectionism in me at a very young age. I recall being a young teenager and having a conversation with her about my perfectionistic tendencies. I am not sure I fully believed her at the time. My perfectionism does serve a purpose: it helps me work towards certain goals in life and not give up. Also, it has assisted me in getting to the point in my life that I feel confident in my abilities as a physiotherapist. Plus, it motivates me to learn and grow.

What is the cost of striving to be perfect, though? The shadow side to my perfectionism is the lack of self-worth that manifests if I have not achieved something in my life (that perfect relationship, for example). Another negative aspect is the lack of self-acceptance that ensues. This is a huge cost. If we are not able to accept ourselves for who we are, we rely on others for acceptance and approval. If we don't get it from others—or if they take it away—it feels like a huge hole, an emptiness in the heart.

I was searching for that soul mate love we are told we all should have. I was seeking to live happily ever after with that soul mate because I believed I would not be good enough otherwise. My angel card stated: "You are a perfect child of God, and every part of you is wonderful ... You are much too hard on yourself ... Although you enjoy having high standards, it's important to view yourself through loving eyes ... See yourself through your angel's eyes and you will see someone who is a perfect and holy child of God."[1]

We are asked to love ourselves unconditionally. The challenge for me is to detach myself from the outcome because the fastest way to make God laugh is to tell him your plans. When you can't detach from outcomes, all you do is strive to make things happen—it is that "always striving, never arriving" issue talked about in the Tao.[2] It is my ego self that strives for perfection. It is the ego part of my self that tells me I am not good enough until I reach a certain point in my life. Until I have the successful career, enough money, and the perfect relationship, my ego says I am a failure. I will never be good enough if I continue to look at my self though the eyes of the ego. I will never reach that point of self-acceptance. I will continue to strive and never arrive.

A question that I have started to ask myself is as follows: "What would love do?" (Robert Holden, Shift Happens talk radio).[3] When I can answer that question honestly, I know that I am letting go of my ego's desires and making the choice from a place of God-like love.

CHAPTER 5:
THE FEAR OF LOSS
AND BEING ALONE

My first, real, long-term relationship, as a young teenager, was on again, off again. Any strife or disagreement and we would break up. When the disagreement was resolved, we would be get back together. I learned very early on that if you were not perfect or things were not perfect, the other person would or could just leave. Therefore, I always strived to keep everything perfect. That is another one of my holes that I fall into with regards to relationships: doing things for the other person out of fear that the person will leave. I aimed to please. If I really cared for the person, the pothole became even more dangerous.

The princess loved the feeling of being in love. Whenever she felt that way, she did not want to lose it. The shadow of fear of loss would creep in and smother the love. The love was unable to breathe and flourish on its own.

The fear of loss (that comes from change) has kept me trying to hang onto what was special in a relationship. Life is dynamic, like a river flowing. It is never the same. It changes second to second. However, I have always liked the feeling of consistency. Sameness feels comfortable and safe. I wanted my relationships to last forever and be more consistent—like a lake, not a river that is flowing. Even when a relationship was no longer serving my highest and best good, I did not want to let go. I feared that I would be swept away, down river to places unknown. I did not want to be alone. Yet hanging on left me feeling stuck in the mud as the river changed around me.

"What you think about, you bring about."[1]

When you think about loss, that is what you attract—and that loss can come in the form of money or relationships. My picture is like this: things are going really well in a relationship; I feel happy and content. I want this feeling to last forever because it feels so good. This is where I want to be. Instead of being grateful for everything I have at the moment, my mind shifts to worrying about losing everything that I have. This change in what I am thinking about starts to affect my feelings and my behaviours. The thoughts cause jealousy, and that feeling causes me to hold on tighter to the other person. The more I hold on, the more the other person wants to be free. It becomes that self-fulfilling prophecy. Things start to happen that confirm what you were thinking. We never stop to think that we are creating and attracting these things into our lives. Why would we attract the bad stuff? Too often, we focus on what we *don't* want (and not enough on what we *do* want).

The fear of being alone is a partner to this fear of loss. This has worked both ways for me. I have stayed longer in a relationship because I did not want the other person to be alone. Also, I have tried to keep the relationship together by doing what I thought the other person would expect of me. Relationships built on a foundation of obligation, guilt, and expectation will eventually succumb to the outside forces of nature. They are not structurally sound.

Letting go and allowing life to flow has been one of my biggest and most challenging lessons to date. It's hard to recognize that I do not have control over certain aspects of my life. The Tao talks about not being able to grip the water and cupping the water instead.[2] When I have tried to grip and hold relationships tightly, they slip through my fingers like the water would. Cupping my relationships to me means learning to love unconditionally, not loving from a place of "what can the other person do or give to me". These things include time, attention, and affection, and I have tried to use them to fill my own voids. I've tried to use them to make myself feel special. Loving unconditionally, to me, is learning to love as God loves. Not being loving to receive love, be liked, or be accepted; rather, loving from a place in the heart that really wants the best for the other person. I'm talking about love, peace, and joy.

The beautiful princess felt vulnerable and isolated whenever she was alone. There are those who find peace in the solitary moments in life. She was not one of those people. She adopted a lifestyle and made choices that prevented her from being alone. If she was alone in her castle, she could feel her heart crying to be free of the dungeon that was keeping it safe. If she was alone, she would hear her thoughts telling her how unworthy she was.

CHAPTER 6:
KNOW THYSELF

As mentioned previously, understanding what is motivating your behaviours is a great step towards changing them. How well do you know yourself? I was reading books on personal growth and development, but what was I learning? Was I applying what I was reading? I did to some degree, but not the full extent of my potential.

It takes time to get to know your self. I was spending my time keeping busy with my career and trying to help everybody else. I was aware that, when I meditated, I had better days, but I did not meditate consistently. It really was not until I started to study the books and answer the questions that were asked in a journal that I started to get to know more about myself. Prior to the shift that occurred when I was thirty-eight, I had integrated the lessons from the books that helped me with my career goals, but I had not incorporated the lessons that would help my personal, spiritual self.

One of the books that helped me in understanding myself was Caroline Myss's *Sacred Contracts.*[1] In this book, she speaks of Archetypes. Carolyn describes the Archetypes as your energy guides to your highest potential. In her book she describes the four Archetypes that we all possess (the inner child, the prostitute, the saboteur, and the victim). She also states that we have eight other dominant Archetypes that are more unique to each of us. I tend to think of my Archetypes as my dominant personality traits. I did not just read Sacred Contracts, but rather studied this book and the Archetypes. Then I selected what I thought applied to me in an effort to try to understand myself more. What I do, and why I do the things that I do.

Here is my list of what I think are my dominant Archetypes:

1. **Inner child—magical**
2. **Victim**
3. **Prostitute**
4. **Saboteur**
5. **Samaritan**
6. **Servant**
7. **Avenger/Protector**
8. **Teacher/Mentor**
9. **Heroine**
10. **Healer**
11. **Lover**
12. **Companion**

The magical inner child is the part of me who believes in happily ever after and things working out for the best. It is, of course, this magical inner child who cries at sad movies and gets disappointed if life does not seem to be working out like the fairy tale. During the times of struggle, I try to say the following to my magical child:

"Things work out for the best for those who make the best of the way things turn out."

—*Vince Lombarde*

"This too shall pass."[2]

—*Eckart Tolle*

"The universe is conspiring in my favor."

My magical child helps me to have faith in the good and beauty in all people and things. And the magical child contributes to my belief that anything is possible. This is where my imagination lies.

The victim personality tries to keep me safe and secure. My victim tries to keep me from being a victim. I often can become a victim by not speaking up for myself and ignoring my intuition. This is also the part of me that wants to blame others when things don't work out the way that I would like them to, the part of me that does not want to take responsibility for what I attract or do not attract into my life. It is in learning to forgive myself and others that I release the shadow part of my victim. My victim is my sense of justice. She wants revenge for harm done, but it is that part that will keep me suffering. The princess had victimized herself by locking her heart in a cage and thinking that someone would come along—another prince—and rescue her and her heart. And then everything would be better.

And then there is my prostitute. My prostitute compromises my true self for some other gain. She sees something or someone she wants, and she is willing to sacrifice the self in order to get it. The beautiful princess desired intimacy, affection, companionship, and connection with others, so she would sacrifice doing the things that she really wanted to do in order to be with the other person. The beautiful princess would become overly available in the relationship at the expense of her own true needs.

Have you ever put off going out with other friends when asked because your partner *might* decide that he or she wants to do something with you? You don't want to make plans with other people in case the opportunity to do something with your partner comes up. This is the disconnection from others that happens often when new relationships form. Again, this happens because that new relationship is filling a void within you. When making choices for yourself, you can ask the following:

How does this fit with fulfilling my highest potential?

My saboteur likes to point out my faults and unworthiness. She fears failure and not being good enough. She can hold me back from pursuing my highest potential. When the princess became aware of this part of herself, she discovered the key to her self-esteem and empowerment. She retired the dream of having another person build her a castle of self-esteem and acceptance. The beautiful princess discovered that she was giving her power away to others, and she resented it when they did not live up to her expectations. If she listened to her saboteur, she would feel she was not good enough—the fear would hold her back. The beautiful princess, unfortunately, had placed the saboteur as a guard at the dungeon in which her heart was being kept safe. Any potential suitor for the princess had to make it past the saboteur. The suitor had to be willing to capture the beautiful princess's heart. Persistence would be the key because the saboteur was a mighty adversary and great protector.

The beautiful princess's Samaritan offered help to others in need. The Samaritan suggested that the princess make herself available to others. Sometimes, she would help others before helping herself. When it came to matters of the heart, the princess would often channel a great deal of her love and attention into one person rather than focusing on helping the whole. At times, her love for helping others became more exclusive rather than inclusive. What she needed to learn was how to love everyone like she loved one, to recognize everyone's desire to be included and feel special. The princess wanted to empower others not disempower others. She had to be careful not to do too much for others.

Everyone has the potential to grow and learn through their struggles and challenges. I have learned that it is not up to me to control their experiences. I can let the person I love know that I am available if they need me, and I can wait for them to ask for help. This involves me paying attention to my intuition in terms of when to intervene.

"You can go through pain or grow through pain."[3]

—*Robert Holden*

The beautiful princess was also a servant, and she made herself available to others for the purpose of enhancing their lives. She saw it as her mission to add value and make a difference in the lives of others on a daily basis. Her greatest challenge was to practice enough self-care so that she was not consumed by the needs of others (at the expense of *her* self). Her servant could feel less than adequate compared to others. The servant self is where the desire to please others resides. As the princess awoke to her servant self, she realized where she felt inferior to others. She did not feel beautiful enough or good enough to be considered desirable by the princes. She felt inferior to her male bosses at work. During her awakening, she was asked to take a corporate position that would take her to another land (and away from the people she currently served). The corporate ladder was there to climb, but there was a force holding onto her foot that would not let her climb. She stayed her course, though, because her higher self was guiding her. She felt a sense of pride and strength in knowing that she was being true to her self, her desires, and her passion.

One of the princess's most dominant characteristics was her protector. She is not truly a warrior—she shies from conflict and violence—but she will do what it takes to protect the weaker ones and the ones she dearly loves. It is the protector that will often attract those in need of rescue, the damsels in distress. I am sure there is a male version of this characteristic as well. The challenge becomes establishing a relationship without codependency.

When the princess was just six years old, there was a young knight whom she befriended. His name was Anthony. Anthony would have to sit in the hall in the morning during the Lord's Prayer and Bible reading. The princess did not know what Jewish was or why it was different. She did not understand why Sir Anthony had to be alone in the hall. Therefore, the beautiful princess got permission from the queen mother to join the knight in the hall, stating that she did not believe in God either. In reality, she just did not want her friend to be alone in the hall.

The thought of one person taking advantage of another or hurting another has always bothered me. Where did this come from? Why is it so strong within me? The answers may lie in my subconscious mind. It was during a PSYCh-K session (using Bruce Lipton's *The Biology of Belief* as my guide)[4] that I had a very interesting and strange experience. The following is what I wrote in my journal:

> I went on a course this weekend called PSYCH-K. It is all about tapping into our subconscious mind to discover how we are programmed and making changes in the areas where the subconscious mind is blocking our conscious goals. Yesterday, in class, I worked on some of my blocks in regards to acquiring the wealth that I consciously desire. I also did a self-balance last night before bed (even though it was late). I decided to do another one tonight. I did my Vak to the Furture (before I started to help myself form a belief statement for my net wealth goal). And then I did my belief statement and balanced for that. My subconscious liked the resolution balance (seems to be the one preferred for my money stuff), and again, it was the right brain that was blocking it.
>
> And then I discovered that there was another one that needed to be balanced, but it was not on the sheets. It led me to a book, *Secrets of the Millionaire Mind*[5], which I read in the past and did some work with. On page forty-seven, I found the following statement "I observe my thoughts and entertain only those that empower me. I have a millionaire mind." I

- *Happily Ever Now* -

tested both separately, and both were weak. But it was not okay to balance for these statements yet (I got a pretty clear *no* for both using both methods). Therefore, I stated, "There is another priority statement that needs to be balanced first." *Yes!* It was on one of the sheets, but not the prosperity one that I expected. It was on the self-esteem sheet, number twenty-one: "I am proud of who I am." *No!* This really surprised me. It was safe and appropriate to balance for this (again, with the resolution one). It was my left brain blocking this one.

Therefore, as my hands came together and my body felt like it was really swaying back and forth, my hands stopped midway (in my 20s, it felt like). Not sure what happened here to block this. My body felt like it was moving like a washing machine at this time. And then my hands moved more quickly together until they got really close … and then they stopped. But then they got pushed really quickly back behind me, and again, my body started to shake hard. After that, they came rapidly forward but did not meet. And then, they went back behind my body again. This time, they stayed behind me, and I felt a sword going into my stomach area. I thought I had killed somebody, and then I thought I was being killed—but it was me who was driving the sword into my stomach. I could feel it going deeper and deeper.

I felt like I was doubling over, and the blood was running out of me. There were tears in my eyes, and my breathing rate increased. I was gasping. I felt like I was going to vomit. My arms were still behind me and up, but then they dropped and came together down by my solar plexus. I brought my hands to my face, and it took a few minutes before I was able to lock in. After this, I tested strong for "I am proud of who I am" and "I observe my thoughts and entertain only those that empower me. I have a millionaire mind." There is a lot of activity in my solar plexus right now, and I feel very awake.

It is also interesting to note that, as I am writing this, I am recalling my injury to my solar plexus when I was nine years old (I went into the boards during a hockey game, and the end of my stick was thrust into my solar plexus, which cause me to vomit). It is the same feeling that I am having now. When I was learning craniosacral therapy, the release work to my solar plexus made me vomit when I brought to mind the memory of my hockey trauma. I was so drained the next day.

The solar plexus in the chakra system represents our personal power. This is my area of weakness: asserting my personal power and setting my personal boundaries. My struggles in this area have to do with not wanting to disappoint others, concerns about others not liking me, and the desire for their love and approval. By not having a strong sense and awareness of my personal power (and what I was giving away), I would allow others to direct me where to go, like a sailboat without a captain at the helm. What I am starting to realize is that I am the captain of my ship. The wind might blow, but it is up to me to capture the wind and steer the ship. Keeping my personal power in relationships is going to come from me realizing when I am doing things out of fear of rejection, loss, or the need to be accepted and loved—instead of doing them to be willfully helpful, giving, kind.

When I look back on all the significant relationships in my life, there was a dominance of these archetypes. I tried to save people who were struggling in some area of their lives. Perhaps that is why certain people chose me, for my strong protector qualities. It allowed them to feel safe when they were not feeling so safe. The time may come in each relationship when the drive for freedom, self-reliance, and self-protection takes hold. The other person may desire to break free of the need to have a protector, to escape the castle wall, to go out into the world and explore. This is what Siddhartha (Buddha)[6] did. It did not matter how much his father tried to protect him from the outside world and all of its negativity and despair. Siddhartha had a destiny that needed to be fulfilled. Everyone has their own destiny. Though I am a protector, I cannot try to deny someone the opportunity to grow or learn. The best I can do is to be a bit of a safety net for people—someone who will listen without judgment, someone who will be compassionate and understanding. And I must not try to fix or control the outcome—even if that means so pain might ensue.

The beautiful princess also has strong healer characteristics. Her passion is to serve others by helping them repair their bodies, minds, and spirits. It is her mentor who likes to guide and teach what she has learned, especially regarding care of the castle (the body) and the spirit that resides within the castle walls. I do need to be aware of doing too much for people and not allowing them to discover life for themselves—that is often where the best learning happens. I am merely a guide or a resource.

The heroine inside of the princess is on a spiritual quest for inner knowing and self-empowerment. It might be this heroine who is the dysfunctional independent person (DIP), according to Robert Holden[7], but she is learning to receive help from others on her mission.

The princess is also very much a lover. She creates very strong heart connections. She is very passionate about life. She experiences joy when doing what she loves. When working with others as a therapist, it is the connection with her clients that matters the most. When spending time in nature, she feels connected to a world much greater than herself. When she writes, she feels connected with the universe and God. The lover aspect of the princess was hidden away for protection and not always shared due to the princess's fears. These fears include rejection, not being good enough, and not being beautiful enough. She never felt beautiful enough for a handsome prince.

The princess is very much a companion. She displays a strong sense of loyalty towards all those who she cares about. She will be available for emotional support or other support as needed. The princess does need to be aware of when this loyalty to others is coming at a cost to her self, though.

It is through knowing yourself and being aware of what drives your behaviours in relationships that you can step around the potholes that you might encounter. Caroline Myss stated that these Archetypes are part of who we are. She said that they guide us to live our lives in certain ways. I don't want to look at my living to serve and protect others as a negative quality. These are part of me and who I am. Because I have spent time getting to know and love myself, I have become quite proud of these parts of myself. I love these parts of myself—most of the time, anyway ... when they are serving me well.

I have to be aware of both the good aspects of who I am and the shadow sides of my Archetypes. I need to be aware of when and where I have attached part of my self-worth onto my ability to make another person feel happy, content, secure, safe, and loved. What am I if I cannot make another person feel good, happy, content, loved, or secure? I feel like a failure because I have not been able to fulfill my role. And then I feel rejected. I need to be aware of when I am doing too much for another and disempowering him or her. Awareness also helps me recognize the situations when I am giving in, in order to have another person fulfill an area in myself that I am not filling on my own.

The beautiful princess desired that happily ever after, romantic, Prince Charming, with whom she could ride off into the relationship sunset. She wanted to feel important and special. In order to attain those goals, however, she would have to give her power away.

I want to climb a tree
and sit where no one else can see—
to be safe as I look down
on the world down there below me.

I want your arms around me tight,
I want to be with you all night—
to be safely wrapped in your love
just to know that I'm all right.

It is through the understanding of ourselves that we are better able to be authentic in our relationships with others. Such understanding requires work to move beyond the mind and emotions to the interior of our soul (Carylyn Myss, *Entering the Castle*).[8]

CHAPTER 7:
GIVING AWAY YOUR POWER

When you allow other people to fill the voids in yourself, you are giving away your power. As you give away your power, you start to feel inadequate. This might lead to resentment towards the other person because it feels like that person is taking your power. As resentment builds, the relationship becomes less and less stable. This giving away of our power often happens at an unconscious level, until we become aware of when we are doing it. Without knowing it, you can take away another person's power by expressing your love in a certain way. In loving another and wanting to make the person's life easier, I do things for them that they could do for themselves. This happens in my friendships as well as my relationships. It is through my awareness of when I do this that I will be able to stop doing it.

It has been said that expectations are the downfall of every relationship. Relationships involve energy exchange, and many have compared such exchanges with making deposits and withdrawals at a bank. We exchange energy just like we exchange currency. We make deposits to each other when we are present for them, when we say something loving and kind (but not just something that is aimed at feeding the other person's ego so we can get something in return). We make a deposit when we do something to help another person. Soulful love comes from the heart; it is unselfish and given without expectations.

When we do or say things out of a sense of obligation (or as a means to get something for ourselves: time, attention, affection, security, love, or money, for example), it ends up being a withdrawal from ourselves and the relationship. The withdrawals happen when we take something from another person, such as taking energy without asking or for selfish reasons. This action can come in the form of putting the other person down (belittling him or her) because we don't feel good enough about ourselves. When I feel attacked, my soul retreats in defense. It does not want to attack back in order to defend itself. It does put up walls and barriers as protection, though. It does not want to take from the other person—even though it feels like something is being taken from it. The challenge in these situations is to extend love rather than run and hide. For someone else who tends to attack back, the challenge is to extend love rather than attack. Wayne Dyer introduced me to the idea of ending in love.[1]

Caroline Myss describes giving away your power as an energy leak.[2] It is like we have been sliced open and the energy, just like blood, is leaking out. One of the things that Caroline asks us to consider is whether we would continue putting money into an investment that was losing money all the time. The answer is no. Why, then, would you continue to put time and energy into a relationship investment that was losing all the time? A situation in which things are constantly being withdrawn but no deposits are being made is toxic. She tells us that it is when we have spent all of our energy for the day (sometimes within the first ten minutes of the day), we have to get more from somewhere. Either you end up taking it from someone else, or you take it from your physical being. When you start taking it from your physical self, the disease (*dis-ease*) process starts to occur.

It was only in a recent counseling session that I discovered that my feelings of frustration with a relationship had to do with unfulfilled desires. The counselor took me below the surface of the frustration. For me, it is often the desire for a heart connection with another person. But the other person, for whatever reason, is unable to fulfill that desire. I was seeking something that could not be obtained from that relationship. By continuing to seek it, I was losing power every time there was contact with the person. And still, the need was not fulfilled. I was advised to release the desire and grieve the loss of the connection that may have once been there. In this way, I am healing the leak. That energy cannot flow from my body and leave me feeling exhausted. The healing, for me, took awareness that I gleaned from a counselor.

The beautiful princess, in her journey to the centre of herself, asked why she did not feel whole. What did she feel was missing in her life that caused her to try to fill it with power outside of herself? She wanted to find her own power. During a meditation and consultation with her spirit guides, an angel card on power presented itself to her. It read as follows:

"You now allow yourself to express your power. Being powerful is safe for you, knowing that you express your power with love. You have all the power of your Creator, within you. All the power of divine love, wisdom, and intelligence is available to you. You have the spiritual power to see angels and the future. You have intellectual power to tap into the universal wisdom of the One Mind. You have emotional power to empathize with others, and physical power that is truly unlimited.

The angels ask you to give them any fears you may have connected with being a powerful person. Your angels see a quiet and beautiful aspect of your true power, stemming from the only power in the universe: Divine love. Allow yourself to shine with this radiant love so that your true power can radiate out into the world in miraculous ways."[3]

The princess had denied her true power. She was doing what was expected of her or what she felt she needed to do to please others—often ignoring her own needs. Part of this was out of fear of not being accepted or loved for who she was. Part of this was out of fear of conflict.

In order to feel whole and true to herself, the princess recognized that she needed to acknowledge and accept her own power from a place of love. She needed to forgive herself for the times when she gave away her power or took someone else's power.

It is through loving and accepting herself that she started to discover the power within herself. The princess also had to be aware enough to recognize when she was compromising her own needs for the sake of avoiding conflict or pleasing others. This takes honest communication with yourself and others.

Carol McCloud has written a great book for children, *Have You Filled a Bucket Today?* [4] Every adult should read it too. She says that we all have an invisible bucket, and it has the following purpose:

**"[To] hold your good thoughts and
good feelings about yourself."**

Chapter 8:
Living without Regrets

As I have grown and looked within myself and at some of my fears, I have come to the conclusion that..

I am not afraid of dying,

I am afraid of not living.

What are you most afraid of? When I was a young child, I was afraid of the dark and the monsters that lived in the closet and under the bed. I wish I had gotten to know Sully from *Monsters, Inc.*[1] back then. To this day, though, I still like to sleep with a candle lit and my closet door shut.

As I began to care more about what others thought of me, fear of failure became a huge road block. It would clasp my feet in chains and keep me from moving towards anything that was unknown. I feared not being good enough. Fear of heights (which manifested later in life) would keep me from experiencing new things or seeing the beautiful world from a different perspective. Fear of rejection would prevent me from getting to know another person.

Nobody wants to feel disappointed or rejected. We all want to remain safe and comfortable. Walls of fear create the illusion of safety, but they are really a dungeon, restricting our freedom to living up to our highest and best potential. There are two phrases I heard from Wayne Dyer[2] that I continue to refer back to:

"Don't die with the music inside of you."

"Don't die wondering."

The beautiful princess wanted to please others in her kingdom. When she saw others were pleased with her, she felt loved and accepted by everyone around her. This was shadowed by an underlying fear that, if she failed, she would no longer be loved.

Where do we get these thoughts? It is not as though my parents were neglectful. They were both kind, loving, caring, and giving. Just to show you where these "mind viruses"[3] can come from, I think the need to please (in order to feel loved) stemmed from what I felt I got attention for as a child. My sister was sick as a child, and my brother was adopted when I was four. He had some behavioural issues. My brother delivered what we called cold pricklies from *T.A. for Tots* [4] in order to get attention. Resorting to "cold pricklies" means using negative behaviour to get attention (as opposed to employing "warm fuzzies", or positive contributions, to get attention). I was a warm fuzzy kind of child. I only know this from reflecting back to when I can remember things, but I know that I got (and still get) positive attention for excelling at sports, academics, and demonstrating appropriate behaviour. When people point out my shortfalls—areas where I am not measuring up—I take it very hard. I don't feel good enough, and I have a tendency to take such criticism personally.

It is truly amazing what we can discover when we look back on the events that we recall from our past and link them to how we are feeling in the present. Looking back can help explain why we react or respond the way we do in various situations and circumstances.

There was an expectation that I was a good kid and always did everything right. At least that was my perception of it. Thus, by being good and pleasing others, I was loved. Who in their right mind would want to do something that they might fail at? I had to be perfect so I could be loved. If I was the perfect person (exactly what the other person needed), that person would not leave. There is also the issue of being rejected. If someone else rejected me, I would not feel perfect or good enough.

If there was a chance that there would be failure, I would avoid doing the activity. The unfortunate part about this is that I might live with regrets, die wondering, and take all my hopes, dreams, aspirations, and creations with me.

Living beyond the fears (and out of my comfort zone) required faith in a purpose greater than myself. Acting in spite of fear was not an easy task, though. In a recent discussion with Clemens Rettich (a business coach), we talked about having faith during periods of transition. I told him what I had heard Robert Holden [5] say in regards to the *Indiana Jones* movie where the protagonist must take a step across a gorge despite there being no visible bridge. He had to believe first and take the step before the bridge appeared. Clemens used the analogy of the trapeze artist:

"At some point you are going to have to let go of the first bar so you can grab the second bar. And in that moment you will be in mid-air, without anything to hang onto. Yet that moment is required if you want to do anything more than swing back and forth on that first bar forever." [6]

"You must let go to grow." [6]

There was one area of my life where I rarely felt fear: playing ice hockey. I felt confident in my abilities to contribute to the team and get the job done. It did bother me when I felt I let the team down, did not play my best game, or did not score enough goals. This confidence did not follow me off the ice and into my personal relationships, however. Off the ice, I never felt good enough socially. My athletic ability is what got me accepted—at least that is what I thought.

I worked hard to get good grades in school, so I was accepted for that as well. It seemed like it was expected of me because I was the daughter of a teacher. How would it look if I did poorly in school? Even when it came to my career, I poured myself into my education and learning until I got to the point where I felt confident in myself and my abilities to truly make a significant difference in the lives of the people who came to see me. It is not that I have to feel like I am the best; rather, it's that I have to see myself as having enough worth to contribute to the other person or the collective group. It comes down to feeling internally valuable to the whole.

What are your fears? How do your own fears keep you safe? How does this affect who you are and what you do in your own relationships? When we choose to live life through our fears, we are choosing not to be authentic. When we choose out of fear, we choose not to love. When we choose fear over love and authenticity, we are choosing to give up happiness and joy. After all, happiness and joy are love and authenticity. When we choose fear, we do not grow.[7]

CHAPTER 9:
THE END OF THE FAIRY TALE

Once upon a time is how fairy tales begin. They all end with *and they lived happily ever after*. In the middle, though, there is always a conflict and something that has to be overcome. Not everyone gets what they want in a fairy tale story—not the bad guys, anyway. There are life lessons woven into these childhood fairy tales.

> **"Positive thoughts have a profound effect on behavior and genes but only when they are in harmony with subconscious programming"**[1]
>
> *- Bruce Lipton*

In other words, positive thinking is a load of crap if our subconscious mind doesn't believe it. We just can't think happy thoughts in our conscious mind and have things change if our more powerful subconscious programming says otherwise. The beautiful princess who wanted to get married could say to herself that she was a worthy, whole, loved person—even if nobody wanted to marry her. She could tell herself that she was worthy of receiving love. But unless her subconscious mind shifted, her conscious input didn't matter. And her subconscious programming began when she was a young child watching all the Disney shows where the desirable girls got married to the princes and the undesirable girls ended up being old hags. Remember: she did not see herself as a girly-girl princess. Did you ever see a wicked witch who was married? Even in *Alice in Wonderland* (2010 version) [2], the lady who was waiting for her prince to arrive was a scattered, crazy, weathered lady. Alice was being told that she should marry the guy she did not want to marry otherwise she would end up like her crazy aunt.

The idea for the title of this book actually came from the thought that our beliefs about relationships are programmed as young children. *Happily ever after* is a common theme in fairy tales and Disney movies. Don't get me wrong, my magical child loves happy endings and cherishes that theme … and I love Disney movies and fairy tales. And many others do, too, based on the prevalence of the happily ever after theme I saw the last time I went to Disneyland.

How is it that I—someone who had wonderful, loving, supportive parents and several loving friends and acquaintances—want more? Why is it that there can still be a feeling of loneliness because I don't have that one special person with whom I have a romantic, special, intimate relationship? The answer to this can be found in how I was feeling as I watched the World of Color show at California Adventure one night. At the end of this beautiful show, they showed all the Disney romantic, happy endings. Snow White found her prince; Sleeping Beauty was revived by her handsome Prince Charming, Cinderella found her prince, and Bella found someone she loved (whom she transformed into the perfect man). Who would not want to be with someone who treated his partner like she meant everything in the world to him? Who would not want an attractive, charming, kind, and caring prince?

As a society, we celebrate marriages and anniversaries. My own parents will have celebrated their fiftieth wedding anniversary by the time this book is published. My friend's father expressed a huge sense of pride in the fact that his daughter was married. Fathers' dreams for their children often involve walking their daughter down the aisle or dancing with their daughter at her wedding. There are huge expectations around having the perfect wedding and marriage. There is a belief system out there that there is something wrong with those of us who are still single (beyond the age of twenty). I was told by an elderly man that life was passing me by because I was still single at the age of forty-five. The truth of the matter, though, is that I live a really full and enriched life.

So with all of these subconscious programs running in our brains (loaded with viruses), how do we stand a chance? You can focus on what you don't have in your life, on what is missing, on what you want. However, every book that talks about manifestation talks about focusing on being grateful for what you have. This helps you change your vibrational frequency. It's like changing the channel on the radio—if you don't like the song, find one you do like.

Okay, so the change part is not always easy. But this is where you stop and think about things you can do for yourself that can shift your mood. For some people, it is putting on a favorite piece of music. For others, it could be exercise (running, walking, lifting weights, doing yoga). It could be writing a poem or journaling; it could be playing a musical instrument or listening to your favorite Hay House radio talk show. Personally, I keep all of those tools in mind. And when nothing else works, a good cry can help.

Crying is a way to release emotion. Living out here on the west coast, in the earthquake zone, we know that little tremors are a good thing because it reduces the risk of a big earthquake striking. We can do the same thing with our emotions. If we try to ignore the emotion, the pressure will just build until it explodes. Brianne used the analogy of a loaded spring—think of winding the jack in the box but never letting it pop open.

Our conscious mind is creative and only thinks positive thoughts. On the other hand, the subconscious mind responds out of habit or instinct. These habits are learned and programmed into us as children. The videos are made with input from our families, friends, and media influences. It is a programmed response, and the subconscious programming is more powerful than the conscious mind. Try to change a habit and discover how hard it is. It does not have to be hard. You just have to change your subconscious mind—Oh is that all?!

Problems arise with following your instincts when the subconscious programming is made up of untruths. You have to change your subconscious programming once you know what it is telling you. You have to go below the surface to discover your *I am truths*. The princess had to go down into the dungeon of her mind.

During meditation, the beautiful princess had an image of soaring like an eagle over the globe. Her arms were held out in front of her, and she was holding the globe in her hands. When she thought about her new profession and the thought of travel, the energy increased. With thoughts about marriage, the energy flow totally disappeared and her arms dropped back to her sides. She did not know the reason for this. She felt, on a conscious level, that she wanted to marry the prince, but there was something deep within her that knew it was not supposed to be. And with this realization came a sadness. Still, the princess decided to lock this feeling away in the dungeon and forget about it. She decided to go on with life as it presented itself. Was the princess wanting another prince to come in and rescue her heart from the dungeon? Yes, she was. She wanted to feel special and loved, and yet the thought of giving her heart to another left her feeling vulnerable, so she built a huge moat around her castle that made it very challenging for another prince to get in to rescue her. If someone was going to get it, he was going to have to be persistent and work at it.

CHAPTER 10:
THE PRINCESS TRIES
TO RESCUE HERSELF—
INDEPENDENCE

Even though the princess wanted to get married, she also wanted to prepare herself with an education so she would always be able to take care of herself. She never wanted to feel dependent and vulnerable. She wanted to be prepared for a failed relationship. She did not think that, even though she was preparing for the what-ifs, she was not allowing the relationships to be successful. It was while she was getting her education that she met her Prince Charming and fell in love.

Relationships can be so volatile. It just felt safer to be prepared for the what-ifs. I have heard, (though I can't recall in which audio or conference that I heard this), that "The fastest way to make God laugh is to tell her your plans."

"Life begins at the edge of your comfort zone"[1]

How do you prepare for relationships when you only get to control your half of them? There are so many unknown and unseen forces around us that we cannot control. For me, it comes back to getting to know myself. The more I can know myself—my true, authentic self—the more I can be aware of whether I am operating out of love or fear, from God or ego.

I can only control my own self and how I respond to what is occurring around me. But boy, is this a hard pill to swallow!

The need to control every situation comes from wanting to be safe. This is the part of the victim that protects us from being a victim. How does our victim keep us from being a victim? It guards our self-esteem. My victim is the part of my self that feels rejected when I am not treated like the most important person in someone else's life (which is the ego's work). It was the victim part of me that wanted me to become educated and independent in this world to keep myself safe. My victim self contributes to my being a Dysfunctionally Independent Person.[2]

The princess was the middle child, and her older sister needed her parents' assistance and attention because of her illness. The younger brother was adopted into the family when he was two, and he also needed more attention. The princess learned to be independent early in life. It was part of her survival and coping technique. Also, keeping herself busy left no time to face her feelings and emotions.

Again, it comes down to letting go of the fear and trusting that everything is as it should be. It comes down to trusting that you will be okay when you allow things to flow through your life. Life is about having the faith that the right people will show up, the right opportunities will arrive, and you will be safe. Just remember to be awake and aware enough to recognize the right people and opportunities—and be open enough to receiving the help and support that you are looking for.

CHAPTER 11:
PRINCE CHARMING—
FEELING LOVED AND SAFE

At university, the young and beautiful—though she did not yet know she was beautiful—princess met her Prince Charming. She was twenty-two years old. He was charismatic and charming. He had dark hair, and he was quite handsome. The relationship was volatile. The princess felt that if she were able to keep the prince happy, he would not leave. This assumption proved incorrect. This was the same hole she fell into during her first significant relationship. Perhaps it was because Prince Charming—although he did come in and sweep the princess off her feet—did not see himself getting married. The young lady, of course, wanted to keep the man of her dreams. She figured that she could live with the relationship even if it did not lead to marriage. That was her compromise. I mean, really, if you think about it, with half of marriages ending in divorce—and divorce being so costly—why would you want to get married? Was it because of our programmed belief that that is what we were supposed to do? Or is there more to it?

I found this written in my journal but do not know where it came from.

Marriage is
a touching of hearts,
a blending of souls,
a sacred promise
to seek and exalt
only the good
in one another—
accepting all else
with understanding ...
in the name of love.

—*R.T. Cusick*

There was a sense of safety and security when the princess was with her Prince Charming—even though he did not want to marry her. She did feel more whole. It was a false sense of security, though, because of the great cost of trying to please him. There were other princesses who showed an interest in the prince. The princess trusted the prince on the outside, but somewhere deep inside, she did not feel worthy or beautiful enough. Jealousy is an emotion that comes from the ego. The ego is jealous because it feels a sense of loss—it was getting some form of external validation that it was loved and desired. When the attention is no longer on it, jealously arises. The ego might wonder, *What does that person have that I don't have? Did I not do that for you? Am I not good enough for you?* The insecurities that arose showed me that I did not feel good enough about myself. I did not see what I had to offer; I did not know myself. I tried to fill this void with the attention of the other person. The cost of trying to be something for someone else is your authenticity, your true, God-like and loving self.

"You don't get what you want, you get what you are." [1]

—*Wayne Dyer*

When you try to be someone you are not (in order to get something you want), what you get is not in line with who you really are. What you get is only an illusion of happiness—not true happiness.

Simply Me

I am many people,

many people

who are not me.

If I think—

which people do—

I am not

really being me

with you,

I am not a person

conglomerated.

You set me free

from those

who form me,

unconsciously allowing

me not to be them,

but myself.

You do not know.

For that,

I love you.

Deep down, the princess really wanted to be loved and accepted for who she was. This is what we all would really like to have in our lives. The princess did not have the greatest self-confidence when it came to her attractiveness. She still required external validation of her beauty and her worth. If there was no one who was interested in her, she reasoned, it must be because she was not beautiful enough (physically). Below is a quote that I came across while reading back in my journal.

"You know that you have a love of a lifetime when you would still be happy if you had nothing else but the love of the other person."

- unknown

Is this what true love is? The God level of love, where love is really all that matters. This is where we shed the ego love (with its demands and expectations). This is the level of love that will continue past the point of the physical relationship.

Do you stop loving the person because that person, for whatever reason, is not your soul companion or everyday companion? All I can tell you is that, when I truly love someone, I still carry a part of that person in my heart. When I get past my ego feeling rejected and unworthy—and consider what it is like to be truly loved—it does feel like enough. It is a wonderful feeling to be loved by another. It is a wonderful, joyous feeling to know that people care about your well-being, your feelings, your successes, your thoughts, and your dreams. To love another is to want to support and nurture that other person's growth. It really is not about demanding, smothering, stifling, containing—these are all elements of the ego. We demand the other person's attention because, without it, we don't feel loved or worthy. We smother the other person by not giving him or her space to grow and be an individual person, which might come from a fear of loneliness. These things happen unconsciously when we do not know our true selves and are not aware of the unconscious programs that we run (or what our ego is after). These are all things that I have done in some of my relationships.

It is our ego that gives us this false sense of who we are. I know one of my ego's shadow demands is recognition and attention. This, for me, falls under the shadow of greed. It fills the void within me, the void that says I'm not good enough.

A female pastor at a friend's wedding described a relationship like a triangle: the couple is at the bottom, and God is at the top. As each person moves closer to having a relationship with God, the relationship becomes stronger. But along the same lines, if one person develops a relationship with God and the other person is does not, the couple will move farther apart.

Who is God? Fiona Faye wrote a book with that title.[2] Like many others I have spoken with, I have struggled with the term *God* because God is seen as a man floating above us, telling us whether what we have done is good or bad and punishing evil deeds. I love the way Neil Donald Walsh describes it in *Conversations with God.* [3] Picture God as a large body of water, like the ocean. As soulful beings, we are just a cup of water out of that God-filled ocean. We are God beings. We all have this God inside of us, but not everyone realizes it. My mother did—she told me she was God. Wayne Dyer would tell us that when we live from the EGO (Edging God Out),[4] we become further from our God-realized self. It is when we live from the heart (and a place of love) that we are closest to our true God-self.

What I came to realize recently (while discussing this whole triangle relationship with a client) was that God is my authentic self. God is your authentic self, too. And as we move closer to being who we authentically are, we can have closer relationships with others. My relationship with this universal energy has been in development a while.

Truth's Mask

If I were you and you were me,
would we be the same?
For no one is just who they are,
so who are we to blame?

Life is full of mystery,
truth is black and white.
What you perceive as truth at night
looks different by the light.

Within this game, deception—
there are those very few
who find a friend who wears no mask
and stays forever true.

We all wear some sort of mask to hide our true selves because we feel vulnerable without such masks. We are worried about being ourselves for fear that doing so will violate others' expectations of us. It is only when we can stop living from a place of fear that we can really take off the mask and be ourselves. A good relationship will be one with one whom you can share your innermost thoughts, feelings, and desires. You can share your true self and be liked, loved, and appreciated for who you really are. Brianne continually tells me: "Human looks good on you." By this, she means that, when I take off my mask of perfection and let people in on what I am truly experiencing, (whether it be self-doubt, feelings of unworthiness, or fears of being alone and unloved), it makes me more human, more vulnerable.

What do you believe about yourself? Have you taken the time to get to know and love yourself? Your real self?

CHAPTER 12: SURVIVING TURMOIL AND CHANGE

Memories Wrapped in Gold

Memories wrapped in gold—
around my finger placed—
forever a reminder
never to erase
times of love and laughter.
Taken far away,
gazing at the gold,
longing for the day
when I could see a future
in every day gone by.
Now the glitter of that gold
only shimmers in my eye,
as the sea reflects the moon,
guiding through the night.
So my heart reflects our love,
wrapped in a band so tight.

Memories wrapped in gold—

around my finger placed—

forever a reminder

never to erase

dreams of you and I.

Together, hand in hand,

stored within my heart,

sealed with golden band,

cutting through the distant night.

Love burning as a star

there for you to wish upon,

no matter where you are.

Memories wrapped in gold—

around my finger placed—

an emptiness surrounds me now,

Only you yourself replace.

The process of remembering who we really are is the journey. The princess was no different than everyone else. In her twenties (when she met her prince), she was discovering her personal power (the third chakra represented in the solar plexus). There were times when she felt a great loss of patience and a great deal of anger. She described the need to detox her spiritual body. I believe it is Don Miguel Ruiz[1] who describes this as the warrior stage, in which you begin to figure out that the dream is just a dream. At this stage, a battle rages in your head concerning what you think you need to do for everyone else and doing what you need to do for yourself. In trying to please others, the princess would give away her power.

The path of personal growth and development started with a book, *When You Can Walk on Water, Take the Boat,* by John Harricharan.[2] The book is about how the Creator is trying to work with us if we are willing to listen. As I read the title now, what comes to mind are some of the lessons from the Tao about being humble. I think about the "valleys under heaven."[3] When you express humility, all things will flow to you as the rivers flow to the lower ocean or the valley. The ego was still very dominant in the princess at this time in her life. She was still looking at relationships and wondering what she could get out of them (rather than wondering what she had to offer). The princess's reasons were centred around the following needs:

1. Fear of being alone
2. Expectation
3. Comfort and security
4. Sense of self-worth

The beautiful princess, who wanted to get married and live *happily ever after,* started to feel like her relationship was going in circles. It was going round and around, and she felt like it was moving but not really going anywhere at all. But was the princess listening to the Creator? Not really. She was too focused on getting what she thought she wanted. There is this notion that we are always supposed to be moving towards something other than what we have. And in the case of her relationship with the prince, it was marriage. But Prince Charming did not want to get married because he was afraid of divorce. So now they were stuck. The most challenging part for the princess was the fact that she was very much in love with the prince. She wanted to get married; she did not think about divorce. She wanted the prince to be the last person she was with in her life. She saw it as a forever thing. But if he was not thinking the same way, should they be together at all? Oh what to do? This is another hole that she fell into. She wanted what you she didn't have, and this prevented her from living in the now. Why not be happy with what you have now? Live happily ever now. Enjoy the moments of life's journey—both the highs and the lows.

I can hear Robert Holden saying that, when we are stuck, it means that there is a better way.[4]

Lack of Direction

On the edge,
it is here I stand—
a half torn map
clutched in my hand.
A single trail
through rough terrain
has honoured me
with sweat and pain.
Long golden stalks
beneath blue skies
now dance behind.
Before me lies,
a darkened path:
width, that of two.
I take your hand
and walk with you.
Secure by guidance,
elated by love,
I soar like an eagle
with the peace of a dove.
The sky so vast,
at times alone,
I fly in circles—
no way home.
You are the wind
that carries me
to dreams unknown

and things to be.

I need you near.

I may need more.

Without the wind,

I cannot soar.

On the edge,

it is here I stand …

What was it that was going to "un-stick" the princess?

The Ultimate Secrets of Total Self-Confidence [5] was a book that the princess discovered next. The message that she took away from the book was that any problems she had were her problems. She owned them.

The relationship with the prince ended after three years. The princess was upset, but she did not really believe it was the end. She continued to work on telling herself that she was a whole person. But when you have used the love, attention, and affection of another to fill the void in your life that comes from not believing in your own beauty, lovability, and worth, you feel the emptiness when the other person leaves. Again I am reminded of what I have heard Robert Holden say on his Hay House radio show, Shift Happens.

"You cannot get hurt in a relationship if you were not expecting something from that relationship."[4]

—Robert Holden

The universe seemed to have a plan of its own for the princess. She found a job that was closer to her prince and in the same city where she was going to continue her education. She moved in with another woman who turned out to be the person who helped her prepare well for the required interview to be admitted to the university. Interestingly, the princess had chosen to advance her education because it would be easier to find work with a different profession if she had to follow her prince as he pursued his dream. She was riding in his car, but she was finding a way to make it work for her security at the same time. Yes, it was a life decision based in part on what she saw for the future with her prince.

Life has a funny way of leading you to where you are supposed to be—even when you don't know that is where you are supposed to be. It's interesting to look back from where you are and think about all the little things that happened to get you there. A lot of the times, we are not aware of these synchronistic events as they are occurring. It is because I wanted to be closer to the man I loved (and him not wanting to move) that I met up with the person who helped me get into physiotherapy school. This is a profession that I thoroughly enjoy, and I have been able to achieve my own sense of security. It is also a profession where I feel like I am able to give of myself on a daily basis and serve others (while getting paid for it). This is something that I tell people who are in career transition: figure out what it is that you enjoy doing—something that you would do for free—and then find a way to get paid for it.

> **"Things turn out the best for those who make the best of the way things turn out."**
>
> - John Wooden

Self-confidence was not something that came naturally to me, despite my athletic and academic abilities. I know that my self-confidence was (and is still) lacking in some areas of my life. I still have (after twenty-five years of work on personal growth and development) a strong tendency to seek perfection and a need to feel special, recognized, important, and valuable.

Where did these feelings of lower self-esteem come from? As a young child, I was very much a tomboy. I loved pants, T-shirts, and running shoes. Actually, I still like wearing those things, but I am also comfortable wearing a dress or skirt. I never really thought about dressing like a girl or looking like a girl, but it did hurt my feelings when a group of grade seven and eight students told me that I was not allowed to use the girl's bathroom at school. That happened when I was about nine years old. I was fairly confident in school—except for the arts, home economics (I wanted to take shop, but girls were not allowed to do that when I was in grade school), music, and reading out loud. Reading out loud was the worst thing that I had to do at school. I was afraid of making a mistake when I said the words. Nobody wants to look like they can't do something in front of their peers. This fear, as far as I know, was not present until grade seven. That is when I also started to struggle with my art—it just wasn't good enough. One time, I labored for hours doing some art, staying after class to put in more time. My grade was a B, which to me meant *below average*, and I was devastated.

I also did not feel pretty enough to be considered a catch with the boys. As my teen years progressed and I dealt with having relationships end, I think my confidence in that area diminished. I often felt (while dating the prince) that people would wonder, *How did she end up with him?* Some of his friends had actually asked that question.

How do we gain self-confidence? It does come through our successes and receiving praise for what we do well (rather than being told what it is we do wrong and needs to be fixed). However, ultimately, it needs to come from within ourselves. It is being happy with what we have in life, not constantly focusing on what we don't have.

When you compare yourself with others, your ego will either feel superior or inferior. It is a no win situation. One of the things that I learned from my martial arts training was that it was about where you were in terms of your training that mattered most. If I practiced what I had been taught and attended on a regular basis, I would improve at my own pace. It was not a race to the finish; it was a journey, and I could enjoy each moment that I was training. Why, then, could I not apply this lesson to my relationships? Why was I always wanting what I did not have in a relationship? I wanted more of the other person's time, attention, and affection. I liked the feeling of being held when I was sad or upset. I found this comforting and safe.

The princess would learn many lessons along her journey. The lesson that each of us has our own perspective on life's events first came into the Princess's awareness while she was dating her Prince.. After the break-up, the prince and the young princess (who wanted to get married and live happily ever after) continued to make contact. When he came to visit, she felt like a school girl with her first big crush. He acted like they were still together, but he talked like he was still unsure. In his mind, they were not together, but in her mind, they were together. Who was right? Could both be right?

This message is repeated in the *Fifth Agreement:* we all run our own movies.[6] What we think of ourselves is not how other people perceive us. And what we think of others is not the way that person sees himself or herself in that person's movie.

We also have this same message in another book, *When Everything Changes, Change Everything,* by Neil Donald Walsh.[7] He talks about *"Changing your choice about Truths."* He also talks about reality being what we think is happening, which is based on our experiences, past events, emotions, and thoughts.

He describes three different levels of reality. There is what we imagine to be true. This, he points out, can lead to turmoil because it is not necessarily true, just imagined. This is our fairy tale, the dream or the fantasy of everything being perfect all the time. What exactly is perfect for one, though, is not necessarily perfect for another

"In my life I have spent a lot of time worrying about things, most of which have never happened."[7]

Second, there is our apparent reality, which is what we see as real based on what we know from our past. Last of all is the actual reality—what is actually true. Thinking about this can give us peace of mind. I love the following questions by Elizabeth Kubler Ross:[8]

"Is it true?"

"How do I know it to be true?"

"What would I do if it weren't true?"

Was it true that, because the prince broke off the relationship, he did not love her? Was it true that, because the prince chose not to have a relationship anymore with her, she was not good enough? If she thought either was true, how did she know it to be true? Could it be her perceptions, were merely, a false belief about the truth? Could it be that that particular relationship was no longer serving her highest and best good? Could it be that, in order to grow and do what she was supposed to do in her lifetime, she needed to change? Could it be that she was unwilling to make the change for herself because of her strong desire to be in a relationship to feel safe, secure, loved, accepted, and worthy? However as long as she was in that relationship, she would not discover those feelings from within herself because they were being fulfilled from outside of herself.

Where would she be without the thoughts that she was not good enough, not worthy, and not loved? Happily ever now! What is truth versus illusion? How do you tell the difference? Without the illusion of not being good enough, not worthy, and not loved, the princess would find her peace and joy in the present time. Experiencing peace and joy is evidence you are living the truth and not the illusion.

All this is not to say that the princess did not feel the pain of loss and change. The princess was not aware at the time that this pain came from the ego telling her that she needed what the prince gave her in order to be special. She had not yet discovered the special gift inside herself.

CHAPTER 13:
LOVE VALIDATED—THE
DOGHOUSE THEORY

Everyone wants to feel that they are loved and appreciated. How do we know we are loved? The princess feels loved when the people in her life spend time with her and give her attention and affection. When she is not having this need fulfilled by the other person or people in her life, she retreats. Why does she do this? It is what I call *the doghouse theory.*

When I was a young child, I remember wanting to run away from home when I was angry or upset with my parents. I typically ran away up the street to my friends place. One time, my friend's mother, Joyce, told me I could not stay with them because they had so many children already. What I did instead was hide in the doghouse that was in our garage. The voices of my loved ones could be heard as they searched for me. Although I don't recall what it was that they were saying, I do recall being pleased that they were actually looking for me. Can you imagine how you might feel if you were hiding and no one looked for you? What this meant to me was that I was actually loved and wanted. It validated their love for me.

In relationships, I seek the validation that I am loved by pulling away (either emotionally or physically) when I am not feeling very loved. It is not an action that is intended to be hurtful, revengeful, or spiteful. It is just the way that I use to know that I am still loved and cared for. This action was a very unconscious one for me until recently. A very good friend could not spend as much time with me as I would have liked. I decided I did not want to spend the whole holiday weekend alone, so I went ahead and made other plans. I didn't realize my rationale until we talked about the matter later.

The fear of rejection was a huge area of concern for the princess. But what this fear ended up being was an unconscious form of manipulation in her relationships. The princess was very giving in her relationships, but when the other person did something that felt like rejection (such as not being available) she pulled away (retreated into the doghouse). This tended to cause the other person to feel guilty, and the other person often spent time with the princess out of obligation. Resentment began to grow.

Since recognizing this pattern, I actually feel less of a need to have my love validated. The way to find your self-confidence is to go within. If you don't have a great friend who will call you out on your behaviours (leading you down the path to introspection), try a life coach or counselor—someone with whom you can develop a trusting and honest relationship.

A relationship where the focus is on me does make me feel special. But if I want things to change and go down a different road, I need to feel special and worthy from the inside out. This thought came to me one day while trying to discover what I felt was missing from my life and what I was seeking from a relationship.

If what you seek you cannot find, go within. Once you find it there, you will find it everywhere.

Passion was my answer. I wanted someone who loved me passionately and who would show me this. But I realized I was full of passion.

Chapter 14:
Constant Transformation

The queen was a smart and wise woman, and she often told the princess that there would always be change. She gave the princess a card with the Serenity Prayer[1] when she was very young. It reads:

**"God, grant me the serenity to accept
the things I cannot change,**

The courage to change the things I can

And the wisdom to know the difference."

As her self-confidence grew with karate and reading (*The Ultimate Secrets of Total Self-Confidence* [2] at least three times), her relationship with the prince got more challenging. Karate had introduced her to *mukso* (meditation). She could feel great energy flow between her hands as she meditated.

She took refuge in the thought that, regardless of the outcome, she had grown in the consciousness of love. She was starting to recognize the need to have balance between the body, mind, and spirit, and she knew that the changes in her relationship with the prince presented her with an opportunity to grow spiritually. These changes were occurring naturally.

The princess continued to struggle with her relationship with the prince. They were together, but they were not together. It was a really confusing time. Every time it was more off than on, she would go through feelings of sadness, anger, and loneliness. The loneliness would often come from not having a companion with whom she could share her innermost thoughts and feelings.

There were signs that there was someone else in his life, but when she asked, he denied that fact. However, she later discovered a voice message and a letter that confirmed there was someone else. The distance between the princess and the prince became more pronounced. The princess got work closer to where the prince lived (and where she would be going to school). The prince decided that he would focus on his relationship with the princess again, but happily ever after was not in the stars for this pair. There was more to his relationship with the woman on the other end of the phone.

There was a terrible loss of trust. There was also anger. There was doubt as to what *I love you* meant and what commitment actually was.

The moment filled with silence
when three minds combine,
a darkened path enlightened—
an instant gone with time.

A reflection on the water,
ever-changing face,
then rippled by the stone
kept whole by Kan's embrace.

Adapt to daily changes,
move freely with the soul.
A moment passes quickly,
Survival is the goal.

Kan is from the *Book of Five Rings*,[3] and it is an unconscious force or instinct (God). Basically, I was feeling like, in order to survive, I had to learn to follow my gut instincts. I had to live for today (again, a message that did not sink in very quickly based on my relationship history). Listening to my instincts is something that I was trying to do in my twenties, and I am still working on this skill in my forties. It is not something that is often encouraged. We are often taught that the adults know what is best for us. We are told that we should feel this or that or do this or that. Therefore, we stop listening to our intuitive voice.

Part II:
Climbing out of the Potholes

Chapter 15:
Forgiveness Is the Key

"Forgiveness is the scent the violet leaves
on the heel that has crushed it." [1]

—*Mark Twain*

It was in Robin Sharma's book, *The Monk Who Sold His Ferrari*,[2] that I read about putting rocks in the backpack that you carry with you throughout life. When something happens to you, and you don't forgive the responsible party, it is like putting a rock in your backpack. This can weigh you down over time. Every single book that I have read on personal growth and development discusses the need to forgive others and ourselves.

I have a tendency to hold onto anger—often unknowingly. Not wanting to acknowledge my anger and keeping it repressed came from a sense that anger was a useless and harmful emotion when expressed. It would only cause harm. But repressing that anger—denying that feeling—left it trapped in my body where it festered. I would hold on to anger to justify my feelings of self-pity and rejection. It kept me a victim (and recall that my victim qualities give me the illusion of being safe).

The break-up with the prince was needed. Without it, the princess would have lost her self. She just did not want to let go because he was her first true, soulful love. This is when she put her heart in the cage and locked it. And then she hid the key. Pride was the shield and entitlement was the armor used to block any potential hurt or harm from finding her heart. Wrath was the sword that would ward off any potential suitors. It was ten years later that the fairy godmother, Kristen, discovered the heart locked away in the cage and guided her to the key that she had hidden so well behind the hurt, anger, and grief.

Understanding that forgiveness is the key to healing is only one part of the equation. Learning how to forgive can be a great deal more challenging. The fairy godmother told the princess that, whenever she thought about the prince and his bride, she should send them loving energy. She was also instructed to meditate at the level of her heart with thoughts of a pink rose (the colour for love). *A Course in Miracles,* states the following: "To forgive is merely to remember only the loving thoughts you have in the past, and those that were given to you. All the rest must be forgotten. Forgiveness is a selective remembering."[3]

Remember the good and forget the rest. But forgetting does not mean burying the feelings or shoving them in a closet. The princess recently discovered that she could not bury her feelings in busyness. She had to acknowledge the feelings and allow herself to grieve the loss of the relationship.

CHAPTER 16:
BE FLEXIBLE

You never know what direction your life is going to take you until you are actually there. You may have an idea of where you want to go (such ideas make it easier to travel), but circumstances being what they are, you may end up heading in a different direction. When I think about this, I think about being on a boat at sea. I may have charted my course, but a storm may appear that causes me to change direction. If it gets too rough, I may have to abandon ship—maybe wait for the next one. Maybe I'll decide it is not worth the trouble and pick a different destination.

Another analogy came from my business coach. My coach compared life to surfing. You can do all of the preparation (buying the equipment, taking lessons, getting out on the water), but if there are no waves (not under our control), you can't surf that day. You have to go to where the waves are if you want to surf. But the waves will be different each day.

Life has many twists and turns, and if you don't allow yourself to be flexible, you will break. There is a verse in the Tao that talks about being like a palm tree in a hurricane.[1] Or as Neil Donald Walsh would say, change will happen anyway, so why not make it the change that you want rather than let it happen to you (like being tossed in the waves).[2]

The princess had a dream in which her grandfather gave her a message: *let it happen.* She discovered that, by letting go, she was able to look forward to all the possibilities. Thoughts sometimes get clouded by memories and feelings of emptiness. Through these clouds is a hand pushing us forwards and opening doors to the next stage in life. But the princess was trying to keep one foot in the door behind her to keep it from closing. You cannot walk through the open door in front of you until you let the door close behind you.

Believe

There is an emptiness
inside of me,
a desire to hold you near,
to wrap myself up
in all of your love,
warming my soul,
easing my fears
that things that are
cannot be true—
for you are
so far away.
But the fire that is burning
within my heart
keeps growing
with each passing day.
Trust, I must,
these feelings inside—
not letting my head
rule my heart.
Trust in this love:
so true and so strong
that nothing can tear it apart.

Believe in the dream,

believe in the love

that comes from my soul.

It comes from above;

love is the light

that helps set me free—

free just to let

love be

what it will be

The princess felt alone as she let the door gradually close behind her. There was an emptiness in the pit of her stomach. She wondered whether the love was really just an illusion that she created to fill a need. It was hard to know what to believe in anymore. She was lost, but she was not helpless because she knew that she had the strength and ability to regain control. There was a letting go of the thoughts—what could have been.

There is the saying that everything happens for a reason. The princess believed this, and therefore, she also believed that she had to figure out the reason—especially because there was so much pain involved with the breaking of her heart. The need to avoid future pain in this area of her life was very strong. She wanted to know why in order to stop it from happening again. Until she could figure out why, she avoided further relationships in which she felt vulnerable.

Brianne told me something once that she had learned as she was dealing with a loss. It was that we are breaking all of the electronic connections that our brain has made. When we have thoughts, our brains will hardwire these connections. It is like the event has actually occurred. When we end a relationship, we had thoughts about what would happen (children we would have, trips we would take). These thoughts were real to us. Now they will no longer occur and the connections in our brains short circuit and disconnect. We feel grief, and part of what we grieve is the future that we thought we would have.

The princess had envisioned her life with the prince. They were travelling together. They were living together. They were having children together. They were growing old together. But when the break-up occurred, all of those dreams were shattered, crumbled like buildings collapsing in an earthquake. The structure of her life lay like a pile of rubble upon the ground. How could she rebuild it? Where could she start?

Part of her expectations for the relationship came from outside influences. People told the princess that she and the prince were a good match. They were frequently asked when they would be married. There was an expectation that, after a certain time together, people were supposed to get married.

My grandmother was very worried that I would never get married or have children. So far, she has been right. Should she have been worried? Is it a bad thing to be independent? Being independent does not mean being alone. I was told by my sister (who had gone through the turmoil of the end of a relationship) that the pain felt bigger than herself. But then, gradually, the pain was only as big as herself. After more time, the pain was smaller than herself. Where does the pain go? How do we get in and clean up the mess left after the dreams have collapsed into rubble? How do you pick up the pieces and rebuild?

I will travel as the leaf,
and where the wind will blow,
I will go—
tumbling, twisting,
dancing freely with the wind.
Not understanding
the reasons for
the sudden changes in direction,
but allowing.
Perhaps, someday, gently landing
to form a seed
and begin anew.

CHAPTER 17:
ALLOWING

It has only been recently that I heard the following message: we don't always get to know why things happen the way they do.[1] The basic message is to allow and accept things as they happen. The need to know why (and the pursuit of knowing why) could drive a person crazy.

> **"Muddy waters will become clear if allowed
> to stand undisturbed and so too will the mind
> become clear if it is allowed to be still."**

This quote was written in my journal way back in 1995. I now recognize it as one of the verses in the Tao.[2] Life takes some interesting turns and detours. Sometimes we get lost. What I realize—as relationships in my life come and go or change—is that relationships are like the seasons of life. Each season has its purpose and benefit to the overall whole. Each season is special and unique in it's own way. Each season has things about it that we like and things about it that we do not prefer. Life changes—even if we don't want it to—but that change is *always* what we needed to happen. I don't always like it in the moment, but the universe really is conspiring in my favor.

The lesson for me was that each person has his or her own life and purpose. We each have our own dharma. We meet and interact with other people, help them experience life, grow together, and grow apart. What we have to offer each person at one specific moment in time is special in that moment. Just because the moment changes and the relationship changes, that does not mean that it was not special or unique in that moment. It was likely what each person needed at that time for his or her own personal growth. Looking at the changes that have occurred in my past relationships from this perspective has helped me climb back out of the hole. The first time it took me quite a long time to realize this. Each time I fall into one of the relationship holes, though, it seems to take me less time to get back out.

When I have found a love that goes beyond my ego's needs in a relationship to the level of the soul, the love does remain (although the expression of the love for the other person changes).

There is a love I cannot express.

To express it as I feel it

should only loose it.

I often wonder why I feel this love—

this thought has occupied my mind.

I do not know what I feel is real.

Sometimes,

maybe that is all that matters.

Some people touch our lives only for a moment. At times, these people send you in a new direction (in terms of insight, growth, or development, for example). These are the tow truck drivers of life. All of our relationships, all the people we meet, are gifts from God. God sends us the support we need. We only need to be awake to see them.

I am reminded of the story of the flood. A man was at his home as the flood waters rose. A truck came by to rescue him, and he declined saying that God would save him. As the waters continued to rise, he got on his porch. A boat came by. Again, he declined, stating that God would save him. Later, while on the roof of his house, he declined the helicopter rescue, again stating that God would save him. As he stood in front of God and asked why God had not saved him, God replied, "I sent you a truck, a boat, and a helicopter. What more did you want."

We can choose to struggle as though we were in quicksand, sinking deeper and deeper in despair as we struggle. Or we can choose to stop the fight, let go, and relax. When we do this, we stop sinking. We need to trust that someone will come along and help us out. Accepting help from the universe requires me to let go of my dysfunctional independence traits and open myself to receiving.

Allowing is the tow truck that helps to pull you out of the pothole (which entails holding onto what was in a relationship and not wanting it to change). When we allow ourselves to miss that person and love that person before releasing him or her, we release the past and move forward with love in our hearts. This is the affirmation for pain in the thoracic spine (mid-back, between the shoulder blades) from *You Can Heal Your Life*.[3] This was one area of the princess's body where chronic tightness and pain resided.

**"I release the past and move forward
with love in my heart."**[3]

- Louise Hay

When you think of the person who hurt you, send him or her the love that you are feeling along with some light. When you miss that person, miss him or her before releasing the person with love.

"As negative impressions and memories arise, simply paying attention to them has a healing effect. Subtle action operates by looking, watching, and being aware, but not judging, condemning, or rejecting. The negative imprints of your past are not the real you. They are the scars of experience, whereas the good things from your past are signposts pointing toward an opening. By feeling what love is like inside, you activate dormant impulses of love in the here and now. You signal to the universe that you are open, accepting, and receptive to change." [4]

—*Deepak Chopra*

CHAPTER 18:
THE UNIVERSAL KICK IN THE BUTT—ACCEPTING CHANGE

So what happens when your life is not going the way that you think it ought to go? What if you want to change it but keep coming up with excuses for why you don't want to change or can't change. Sometimes, the universe steps in and gives you a good, swift kick in the butt to help you make the changes. This is what we think of as suffering, but in the end, it turns out to be the necessary motivational factor for change.

Neil Donald Walsh states the following:

"Change is always for the better."[1]

"Change occurs because you want it to occur."[1]

When the prince entered the life of the princess, he taught her what it was to be loved. He helped her grow into the person that she became through her experiences with him. She learned to trust—and then to lose the trust. It was not that she did not fully trust him; rather, she no longer trusted what the words *I love you* really meant. She discovered how awful a broken heart felt. The prince told her once that everyone needed to have at least one broken heart. She did not understand why this needed to be so. The fairy tale did not seem to be having a happy ending, and she felt the loss of her magical child-like innocence. She learned that what appeared to be real and true may not be so. But every ending has a new beginning.

Learning to accept change—and not trying to understand it at all times—is another lesson to help you out of the pothole.

Both allowing and accepting change (as a way of healing) are really about surrendering and giving up our need to control our destiny and outcome. It is listening to the divine guidance that we are given. We still have free will, but we get to choose whether we serve our ego or our higher purpose.

Changing Times

They say that autumn is for change,
that fading colours do derange
the way the sun reflects the sky—
the sunsets all now say goodbye
to summer nights
walked hand in hand,
an emptiness
throughout the land.
The wind now blows throughout the night;
the leaves all dance with such delight
at being free to fly around
and never knowing where they're bound.

The autumn sun had left the sky,
the colours left to slowly die.
Covered deep beneath the snow
where silently they slowly grow
becoming green
throughout the spring
to take away
winter's sting.

Autumn's change has now drawn near,
the days do dwindle, and I fear
the time has come for you to leave.
Before you go, you must believe:
the change for me
is everyday
I love you more
that's why I say
That like the leaves beneath the snow,
my love for you will only grow.

CHAPTER 19:
YOUR INNER VOICE—FINDING
IT AND LISTENING TO IT

Change keeps the soul from becoming stagnant. The downside to the change is that, sometimes, it can leave you feeling lost, like you are being tossed about in the rapids or caught up in a hurricane. You get blown off course rather than choosing to change direction because you ignored the message that things needed to change. You ignored the warning signs that the storm was coming or you just decided you could tough it out. Either way, you are now off course and feeling lost and (often) alone.

Do you want to go in a totally different direction? Of course, you ask yourself how everyone else in your life is going to react or judge you should you change your course. This may be where you ignore your intuition and decide to do what you think everyone else expects of you rather than what you want for yourself. Or maybe the storm was strong enough for you to decide that you do need to change course. This is the kick-in-the-butt feeling. Something happens that forces you to decide that you can no longer stay the course.

I was watching a video by Caroline Myss in which she was going through the chakra system.[1] She was saying that when we decide to make the change from the upper chakras, our angels will sit up and take notice. When we are making choices from the lower chakras, our angels do not give us their full attention. What I call *the universal kick in the butt,* she would call our *angels listening to our higher desires and making the universal arrangements to make things happen.* You can leave a relationship that is no longer contributing to your evolution, or your angels will make it happen for you. You can quit your job that is going nowhere, or your angels will get you fired. I am sure you get the picture. This quote found in my journal really stuck out in my mind.

"The footprints of angels are love."

- Unknown

I have a great many angel footprints on my butt. Whenever my life is in the turmoil of change, my fairy godmother tells me to remember the following:

"It is a friendly universe."

"The universe is conspiring in your favor."

"I only deserve the best."

Vince Lombardi stated, "Things work out the best for those who make the best of the way things turn out." Things do work out for the best—even if it sucks in the now at times. But even the sucking part is really just your interpretation of the event. It is really how you look at it. We get to choose how events and people affect us.

Cheryl Richardson said in an interview[2] that life gives us messages. When we don't listen to the messages, it will give us lessons. When we ignore the lessons, we get problems. If we don't deal with the problems, we get a full-blown crisis to deal with. If we listen to and deal with the messages (we have to be awake and alert in order to hear them), we can deal with issues before they become a crisis.

The Princess knew that she had to start listening more to her inner voice. She was able to connect to this voice most often during meditation. Meditation was a way of quieting the mind and allowing the muddy waters to become clear again. There was always a tremendous flow of energy during meditation, and she often felt she received answers to her questions during this time. Mediation was the passage into her subconscious mind and programmed beliefs.

Even though the princess was devastated by the loss of her prince (and vowed to never let her heart get hurt like that again), she felt surprisingly freer. She realized that nothing precious lasted forever. Life was cyclical and ever changing. Everything that composes will, someday, decompose (to paraphrase the Tao).[3]

"This too shall pass"[4]

- Eckart Tolle

It does not matter whether it is something you consider good that is happening in your life or something that you consider bad—it will pass.

It was time to move on, but to where? What would the princess do with all the love that was inside of her? She had a close friend who was helping her deal with the changes that were occurring. (I say *changes* rather than *losses* intentionally). She realized that, in order to have relationships flourish, she should be in them without expectations because expectations were from the ego. But was that possible?

Chapter 20:
Loving Beyond the Ego

How do we love another person without expectations or
without wanting our own needs fulfilled? *A Course in Miracles*[1]
discusses the need and desire for that one special relationship
and asserts that it comes from the ego. It is a relationship that
is exclusive rather than inclusive. The more the relationship
becomes obligatory, the less likely it is to fulfill the wonderful
vision of what true friendship can be. This is much easier
to think about than to actually do. We are having a human
experience, and there are parts of us (as humans) that have
expectations and desires that we want fulfilled. We live in the
world of *ten thousand things*.[2] Still, I believe we should do the
following:

"Be in the world but not of it."[2]

When does the shift happen? When do we start placing
demands on the other person, demands on the other person's
time, demands on the other person's attention, demands on the
other person's love? And why do we start doing these things
that can ultimately destroy the relationship? The princess had
some insight, but she would need a few more kicks at the
can (in terms of close relationships) before she really got the
answers to her questions.

What the princess came to realize eventually was that she
liked the feeling of being with one person because it made
her feel special. She relied on others for love, approval, and

acceptance. The princess thought that being in love was different than loving someone. To love another meant to care about what happened to the other person, but to be *in love* was an action that came out of the emotion of love. She gave love to feel loved. Is it any wonder that no one could live up to her expectation of love in return (while still practicing self-care and self-love)? The underlying yearning for the princess was a true heart connection. When she connected at the level of the heart, it felt like she had also connected at the level of the soul.

But if, according to *A Course in Miracles*, the special relationship was exclusive and separate, what could be said about the concept of marriage?

This marriage vow was taken from Neil Donald Walsh's book, *Conversations with God*[3] and it was modified so I could read it at my sister's wedding. It is the vow that I would like to make to my partner.

> "We often ask the question in today's society, "Why get married?" One reason that is not good is security. Real security cannot be obtained by owning or possessing or being owned or possessed. It cannot be obtained through demanding or expecting (or by hoping that what you think you need in life will be supplied by the other). Real security comes in knowing that everything you need in life—all the love, all the wisdom, all the insight, all the power, all the knowledge, all the understanding, all the nurturing, all the compassion, and all the strength—everything resides within you. And a marriage is an opportunity to give these gifts that you have to the other person so the other person might have them in even greater abundance.
>
> This marriage between [the couple] is a celebration of what is the highest and the best

in each of them, including their love_of life, love of people, love of giving, love of creation, and love of God. Marriage does not produce obligations; rather, it produces opportunities for growth, for full self-expression, for lifting your lives to their highest potential, and for growing towards God through the communion of your two souls."

This is what a true partnership is about, and this can happen between any two individuals. We have relationships with so many people. We touch the lives of more than one person on a daily basis. The quote below was another that I found written in my journal.

"Friendship demands intimacy without ritual …
love without patterns of loving. It does not require
the expression of desire where desire is not felt—nor
will it survive the withholding of genuine response.
Because it is not institutionalized, friendship is
safe from the hazards of daily routines, which
pretending to promote intimacy, defeat it."

—*Carolyn Helbrun*

Looking at both of the above messages, one can see that problems arise when the relationship is based on ego expectations of what a marriage should be rather than a relationship that is based on spiritual growth and development. When we trust, have faith, and let go of the need to control our relationships— let go and let God—life becomes much better.

We are assisted in transforming the relationship from that of the ego's desires, needs, and exclusivity to one with a true and higher purpose. The transformation of the relationship can be one of turmoil. It is often during this transformation period that the relationship is abandoned for another one that fits our ego needs and desires rather than serving a higher purpose. The downside to this is that we often repeat the same lesson with other people.

How does the ego grab onto us in our relationships? When and why is there sometimes a shift from having a friendship without expectations to an expectation-filled relationship full of obligation? For the princess, it all starts when the other person starts to fill a need or void in her life. The void is filled with quality time and attention. When the princess has made a heart connection with a person, physical intimacy will quickly fill a void of feeling alone and undesirable. As that need or void gets filled, there is an increased sense of joy, happiness, and contentment. She falls into the trap of seeking validation and worth from the other person. Any threat to these feelings is met with jealousy and a need to exclude the perceived threat. To allow a relationship to flourish, we need to be aware (there is that *awareness* word again) of the expectations that arise (often from our programmed beliefs) and just let the relationship happen. This is easy to say, but it is much harder to do. I first discussed this idea in 1995, and I still fell into the hole of demanding attention from the other person (fifteen years later). This is because I did not do the work needed to understand the words. When you have another person in your life who will hold up the mirror to help you look within yourself, to discover how you are acting through your subconscious programs, you will grow.

Free Love

Demand not of me

my time and my love—

which is as natural and

free-flowing as a

silver mountain stream,

sparkling in the midday sun ...

like your eyes in happiness.

Do not trap and tame
the gentle deer,
for if trapped, the
beauty disappears.

Let me love you freely.
Lift the coldness
from my heart.
Demand not
and you shall receive.

Trying to hold onto a relationship is like trying to grasp hold of water—it cannot be done. We can gently cup the water in our hands.

Let go of your ego's need for love and allow God's love to fill you. Allow that love to overflow into the lives of others. Ask yourself: *What is the real purpose of my relationship with this other person? Why has God brought us together?* Have faith in God to provide the purpose for your relationships.

Chapter 21:
Outgrow Your Problems

You can't outrun your problems, but you can out grow them.

The princess ended the chapter about her relationship with the prince and started the next chapter in her life. Yet it was not a new book, and she really had not resolved her feelings about the prince and the changes that occurred. Thoughts of the prince still occupied her mind despite the change of setting in her life. The memories and thoughts kept following her. The prince did come to meet the princess before she departed to a land not so far away. He did kiss her, but she no longer felt the spark and tingle that she once had felt.

Suspended

Dare I look upon the night?
So vast, bewildered by the light,
so full of dreams, of hopes, of desires …
of loves rekindled by such fires.
The strength, so softly filtered through
(as though its arms surrounded you,
guiding to a place unknown,
suspended, nailed, through skin and bone).

Dare I look upon the sea?

Beneath it lays uncertainty:
a friend, a foe, the soothing sound.
The waves, so high, come crashing down.
Yet in vain, it draws you near
to wipe away the uncried tears,
to smooth out the jagged stone,
to crush and smother skin and bone.

Dare I listen to the wind?
Through but a crack, it slithers in,
so full of song, the whistle makes—
until so strong, the bows do break.
The coloured dead upon the ground,
and there it helps them thrash around.
New life, with such a gentle gust—
too strong, and all that's seen is dust.

The wind, the sea, the starry night:
all elements of man's delight.
But as with love, so grand and pure,
the power man cannot endure.

There are the good parts about loving someone dearly, and there are the risks of pain, loss, and disappointment should the relationship end. In following the Tao[1], we learn that nothing is good or bad—it just is. There are opposites in life; every force in nature is able to provide us with something positive (warmth from the sun) or negative (skin cancer).

The Princess realized that she was not outrunning the pain that followed. She had to stop, turn around, and face it. She had to get to a point in her development where she could find the strength to ask it, "What do you want?" and "Why are you chasing me?"

When you are not able to let go and grow, ask yourself the following question: *What purpose does holding on to this pain, memory, issue, and anger serve?* We can choose to go through pain or grow through pain.[2] For the princess, she thought that not letting go of the painful experience would keep her safe from further heartache. And it did. But at what expense to herself? What joy did she miss out on by keeping her heart safely locked in a dungeon, by playing it safe?

Initially, the anger helped the princess move forward in her life (as opposed to retreating to a place of comfort and safety that was not serving her highest and best good). But once it had served that purpose, she needed to let go and forgive. It seemed to take forever and a day for the princess to get to a place of acceptance. There has been a lot of personal growth and development to help her heal her broken heart.

A great question that the princess heard from Robert Holden on his Shift Happens talk show was

"Why is this happening *for* me?"[2]

This is a much better question than, "Why is this happening *to* me?" Again, we don't always get to know the *why*, but we can look and discover how we can use the turmoil we are going through. The universe will give you what you need to learn and grow towards your true, authentic self. The universe will help you achieve your highest and best good—whatever that may be.

CHAPTER 22:
ESCAPE FROM THE DUNGEON—
TAKING RESPONSIBILITY
FOR YOUR LIFE

In the land not so far away, the princess continued with another part of her life. She worked on her career. She continued to read and practice personal growth work. Part of her healing came when she looked at the role that she played in the ending of her relationship with the prince. She recognized that her contributing role was her lack of confidence (to be her true self and stand up for what she really desired). Fear of loss silenced her. The prince had moved onto someone who could tell him that he had an ego and was selfish, not someone who always tried to please.

The princess recognized that she had given away her power to the prince. True healing did not start to occur until about twelve or thirteen years after the break-up. Yes, that long. The realization of the fact that she had not healed came from her fairy godmother, Kristen. Kristen helped her see that she had her heart locked up in the cage. The princess cried at the thought—yes, in front of a perfect stranger. She thought that she was over the prince. Apparently not!

Caroline Myss says that a broken heart contributes to a huge energy leak from the body if not addressed and allowed to heal.[1] She also says that forgiveness is the way to mend the broken heart and stop the leak. It is a gift to ourselves. I repeat this quote I heard in the Wayne Dyer CD's from because it is such a powerful message:

"Forgiveness is the fragrance that the violet leaves on the heel that has crushed it."[2]

- Mark Twain

In the book *Mutant Messages Down Under.*[3] it states: "All humans are spirits only visiting this world. All spirits are forever being. All encounters with other people are experiences and all experiences are forever connections ... If you walk away with bad feelings in your heart for another person, the circle is not closed and it will be repeated later in life. You will not suffer once but over and over until you learn. It is good to observe, to learn, and become wiser from what has happened."

In not dealing with her feelings about the prince, the princess had left the circle open. Getting over the loss of love is not an easy thing to do—at least not for the princess. After the prince left, a cage was placed around the heart of the princess. It was made of hard steel. Although she did have a special love for her good friend and companion, it was not the passionate love for which she longed. She tried searching for it. The harder you search for something, though, the more it seems to hide. But the hiding place is great: right in the middle of your heart. How could she find it when she had a cage around her heart?

Roses and Bushes

I have seen the rose with its velvet red petals

hypnotize and lure

innocent feelings.

I have felt that rose, green leaves and stem—

prickly place in my hand,

jabbing the core of my heart.

I have searched. And now, before me, lies
the rosebush:
beautifully blooming like friendship so strong.
No longer will soft petals wither and dry
while nourishing water flows.
I hold in my heart a fully bloomed rosebush.
There is no pain, only love.

What the princess missed in having a relationship was the passion of being kissed and held by someone who never wanted to let her go. She wondered whether she would ever have what she was searching for, and even whether that kind of passion was possible in everyday life. What she did know was that she did not want to lose pieces of herself in order to find that love.

PART III:
AVOIDING THE POTHOLES

As I reflect on what I have written so far—and then contemplate writing about avoiding the potholes—I hesitate and ponder whether I am qualified to even consider writing about how to avoid the potholes. My good friend Brianne teases me about my driving and how I always seem to hit the potholes in the road. She is not the first person to comment on this tendency. This seems to be analogous to my own emotional life. I have read numerous books and I have listened to countless CDs and podcasts that discuss letting go of what is not working and the power of our thoughts.

It seems like it would be easy, right? Just change your thought about something and get a different outcome. Take a different path, and you will avoid the potholes, right? I wish it were that easy. I don't know about anyone else, but when I get a thought in my head—a dream I wish to fulfill—there is emotional attachment on the part of my heart. I don't change direction easily. Having to detour frightens me. I fear not knowing where I am going and getting lost. There is the fear that, if I take a different road, it might not be as good a journey as staying on the road I am on. I can recall playing the game of Life as a child. In the game, there are several forks in the road, and you must choose which to take. We all ended up at the same final destination, but we had different experiences along the way.

If our greater purpose here is to discover ourselves as

spiritual beings and to evolve on the soul level, perhaps there is no wrong or right road to choose. A road filled with potholes could be a harder road to drive, but it might lead to a quicker discovery of ourselves as spiritual beings. The harder path might be an accelerated means of growth.

When I am in the middle of making decisions about which road to take—or trying to let go of the past and move forward with my life—I require an infusion of faith. I require a faith that I am learning what I am supposed to be learning, and growing the way I am supposed to be growing. I require faith that the universe is conspiring in my favor to bring me all that I require to be successful in my journey, and that I am where I am supposed to be … simply because I am here.

I am still learning, just like you are. Perhaps that is what makes this such an interesting journey. As I learn, you learn. What I have to offer is my story—and the rest of the journey to date.

CHAPTER 23:
MIRROR, MIRROR

The quote below was again one that I came across somewhere and wrote it in my journal.

> "We have
>
> grown into one as we slept and
>
> now I can't jump
>
> because I can't let go your hand."

—Marina Tsvetayeva

The princess avoided looking into the mirror for a very long time. Not only was she afraid of the dark, but also of her own reflection. Occasionally, she would glance at herself as she hurried to fix someone else's problem or reach the next achievement. One day, while on the water, the princess met a kindred spirit who seemed to have been sent to help the princess stop, look into the mirror, and reflect. What she discovered was how she behaved in relationships with others. The princess desired to be special and have a significant other in her life treat her like she was special. The princess, therefore, projected this desire onto any special relationship that she had. The world would revolve around the other person, and she would change herself to make that happen. To give was to receive. Receiving that special attention and affection would fill the void inside herself. It was the void of not feeling special without the love and approval of another.

How do you keep your own power while in a relationship but still find a way to feel connected? I picture a relationship where each person maintains his/her own power like being like two separate pillars, each doing its own thing but working together to support the structure (the relationship). If you merged together into one pillar, the structure/relationship would be unstable. I thought this way because it allowed me to view relationships as two people helping each other out while maintaining their independence (power) and still working to support the whole. *Independent* is probably the number one word that others use to describe me. You might even say *extremely independent*. It keeps me safe yet still connected. I get to keep all my power. But really, if I was trying to maintain a relationship by always doing what I thought the other person wanted—no matter how much I tried to not rely on the other person for anything—I was giving my power away.

Recently during a counseling session, the therapist stated that we often loose our individuality in relationships when it becomes like two overlapping circles. Though each circle is a circle unto itself, there is a section of overlap. Where there is overlap, it often feels like there is increased resilience, strength, and support, but this can be an area of dependency. There are areas of our lives where we need help and support. How do I get this without becoming an overlapping circle and loosing myself in the other person? Though I (as a circle) might connect with many other circles (family and friends, for example), I don't have to overlap. I remain a whole, complete circle, but still connected. When I am connected, I am able to give, and I am able to receive.

To be honest, I am still unsure as to which is the best view of the ideal relationship – pillars or circles. Though we are whole unto ourselves, we are not separate. It is the ability to see ourselves as one that makes us stronger.

"Friendship is comprised of a single soul inhabiting two bodies."

—Aristotle

Being able to see and feel myself as whole allows me to stop using other people in my life to make me feel whole (via their approval). When I see myself as whole, I do not have to change the way I act or behave around others to get their approval. If I can see myself as whole and worthy, I will neither compromise myself nor my values. This is how I will be able to keep my power. Trust me, I have to remind myself of this every single day—which is why I journal, read, meditate, and take in personal growth and spiritual lessons. This is my own daily spiritual practice.

To this day, my kindred spirit water guide continues to hold the mirror for me so I can move beyond reading the words in a book and towards reflecting on my own thoughts and actions. This way, I can make the needed changes and grow.

You cannot grow under the shade of another person.

A tree that is taller than the saplings below will take the nourishment from the sun and send it to the saplings below to help them survive. But there comes a time when, in order for the saplings to grow, the big trees must move out of the way.

The princess loves to help people. She attached her self-worth to being able to protect, provide, health, mentor, and guide other people. In wanting to be of service—in order to feel valued and worthy—the tendency was to do too much for the other person. The princess has always been a get-it-done type of person. This means she does not often allow time for other people to do something at their own pace. The princess recently discovered how this can disempower the person she is trying to help. The other person may start to feel inadequate instead of appreciating the help. This tendency to help too much and shadow the other person often comes from a place of love—the princess doesn't want to have the other person experience pain or struggle. To empower another is to allow that person to grow. The princess came to realize that each person has his or her own journey, and the purpose of her relationship with them is to help them discover their own worth and capabilities to achieve their highest and best good. It comes down to the faith and belief that the other person can handle what the universe gives him or her (allowing the person to grow in a unique way).

CHAPTER 24:
HUMILITY

Everything we read in the realm of personal growth, development, or spiritual awakening tells us to look inside. That is the only way you will get to know yourself. And until you know yourself, you can't be yourself or act yourself.

The princess decided to venture into the dungeon. Alone she was not, for she carried a light with her to guide the way. What she discovered was how her fears limited her from becoming her highest and best self.

The fear of humiliation prevented the princess from speaking her truth and being a stronger voice in this world. She feared appearing weak, incapable, or not good enough. She could recall episodes throughout her childhood and relationships in which she felt humiliated for being different. There were times when she felt rejected or not beautiful enough.

Being humble is the power of the soul. It is courage (standing up for a belief) rather than weakness (following the crowd in order to fit in). When I think of humility, I think of love, kindness, softness, water, nourishment, acceptance, compassion, and my mother.

Knowing what will humiliate me and what being humble means to me will help me when choosing which road to take. Why is being humble difficult for me? I have a huge attachment to outcome. It is a matter of pride and pleasing others. If I do well at something, I will be recognized and appreciated for my efforts. Recognition and praise (for me) have been equated with being loved and accepted (fitting in). Striving and making things happen was what I thought I had to do to be successful. When there is a lack of praise or recognition, I have a feeling of rejection or not being good enough.

There is some discomfort in seeing myself as a humble person. Part of the discomfort comes from associating weakness and sacrifice with humility. It's not enjoyable to give up what you want or desire in order to let others get their way while you remain humble and go without. Also, it's not good to be considered a doormat or a pushover.

Be a valley under Heaven, and all will flow to you.[1]

Humility is having the courage to allow life to unfold and realizing that you cannot control every outcome—in fact, you may not be able to control *any* outcome. Humility is of a higher power. Humility is softness, like water. It is ever-flowing and nourishing without being demanding. Humility is accepting, loving, and being compassionate.

Remaining humble yet empowered requires the following five actions:

1. Rejecting the need for approval from others
2. Detaching myself from the outcome
3. Remaining true to my authentic self (of course, I must also look into the magic mirror and get to know my true self)
4. Practicing self-love and self-acceptance
5. Seeing myself truly as an instrument of God

Your list for what you need to do will most likely be different from mine, but creating such a list is an interesting exercise. Just for the record, I have not mastered this list at this moment in time.

CHAPTER 25: VULNERABILITY

Special Box

Lying alone in the
middle,
they saw it.
The *box*.
Just an ordinary
brown box.
So they left it
to be nothing but
a box.
One of them stood alone,
watching
the ordinary brown box
and them.
This one
lifted open the
ordinary brown box and
inside found something
precious and unique.
Could none of them see

that inside is what matters?

Or

would the box not open for them?

When we do not allow ourselves to be vulnerable, we close ourselves off from opportunities. The princess realized that, by keeping her heart in a cage she was hoping that another prince would come along and guarantee her the outcome that she wanted: happily ever after. Until then, she would remain protected from any further hurt. There were a few suitors who showed interest, but the princess was leery and unwilling to risk her heart. These suitors also did not seem willing to take the time to figure out how to get across the moat and into the castle of her heart. They represented the lost opportunities for healing, growth, and self-discovery. She was too afraid to be vulnerable.

Her kindred spirit showed her the error of her ways and guided her from the dungeon out into the world of love and light. The adjustment from darkness to light was overwhelming for the princess. She wanted to proceed cautiously, but there was a spark that was ignited in her heart.

My Heart Dances

Thoughts so frantic

in my mind,

scattered pieces,

tough to find.

Which road to choose—

to love or not …

shattered pieces,

scattered thoughts,

consequences:

a cost to love.

What is the price
I am so scared of?

But my heart,
it dances
with your thoughts
and marvels in your smile.
It flutters in the empty space
of joy and happiness.
It dances with creation
and feels so heaven bound.
For the magic that created you
(for all of us to share)
transcends my scattered, frantic thoughts.
Love is not a cross to bear;
it is for all,
and it's everywhere.

To fall in love again, to be vulnerable was terrifying for the princess.

Today my heart stopped beating.
The pain of your heart breaking smothered my own heart.
There was emptiness within.
And if my heart was still beating,
the echo would have been deafening.

Being vulnerable involves taking risk. Taking risk involves faith. When I allow myself to be vulnerable and trust that love will guide me safely, I get to experience so much joy. When I allow my fears to guide my choices, I tend to struggle. Allowing myself to be vulnerable when relating to other people is a very new experience for me. It feels like I am coming out of a shell and seeing this world for the very first time. There are times that I want to run back into the safety of the cage. When I make the difficult choice to forge ahead, it is life that I get to experience.

I am not afraid of dying, but rather of not living.

Life is precious; life is a gift. We are here on this earth to experience life. Each person who comes into our lives is a gift. The gift does not have to be packaged in a fancy wrapper to be of value. It might seem ordinary on the outside—just like the paper box. When we open up and show our authentic self, people get to experience the essence of our soul. That is where the beauty lies. But I had to be willing to allow other people to see my inner self. I needed to allow myself to come out of my cage and be vulnerable.

Chapter 26:
Knowing What You
Really Want

In Robert Holden's audio book, *Success Intelligence*,[1] there is an exercise in which he gets you to write out what you want. And then you write what you really want. And then you right out what you really, really want. This always makes me smile because there is so much to this exercise. What I take from this exercise is that what we think we want on the surface may not be what we really, really want in our subconscious minds. If we are not getting what we want, maybe we don't really, really want it.

As the princess ventured further into the uncharted territory of her interior castle,[2] she discovered areas where there was conflict between her actions and her desires. Outwardly, she wanted the happily ever after fairy tale romance. But inside, she was afraid to give up her independence. She was afraid of getting hurt, which requires being vulnerable and sharing yourself with another. It was safest, therefore, to date people who were not going to be fully available in some way or another. That way, it would not feel like rejection—just not the right circumstances. She wanted safety and independence more than she wanted a relationship in which her heart was vulnerable.

The desire to feel connected with other people is huge in my life. When I feel disconnected, I really struggle. I am okay with being alone most of the time. Work fills a void (at times) for me, so during the holidays—when I don't really have plans—I occasionally feel very lonely. My biological family lives on the other side of the country, so I only connect with them a couple times a year in person. It seems strange that, at times, there is so little time to connect with the people who want to get together with me, but when I have time, nothing seems to materialize.

Letting go of the desire to be with someone you deeply love is sometimes challenging. It sometimes involves moving beyond the ego's feeling of rejection (if it was not your conscious choice). It involves focusing on the following fact:

This is a friendly universe that is conspiring in my favor.

What that means to me is that, in the long run, it seems to work out for the best. It involves trusting that, when you let go of one thing, it will make room for something new that might be better for you. All of these things are easy to write and put onto paper. It is a completely different story when it comes to convincing your subconscious that the new things are truly better. It is another issue entirely to convince myself of my own self-worth. Someone might look at me from the outside and think, "She has it all together." No one truly knows our inner turmoil unless we let them in. People might be surprised to learn that, on a daily basis, I have to remind myself to focus on what I have rather than what I feel I don't have. On a daily basis, I remind (or maybe try to convince myself) that I am worthy of a soulful, loving, committed relationship. These reminders often manifest in my journals or during my meditation sessions.

Could Have Been

Trapped in a world of love,
suppressing my feelings and desires,
I care too much to hurt you.
Sleepless nights now haunt my darkness—
if only I weren't afraid …
of feeling
of losing all I felt.
Decisions, hauntingly, will linger,
consequences far from clear.
The choice must be,
slowly it shall come.
Not to disturb the perfect balance
created by feelings of love and friendship.
It is perfect, but natural not;
Therefore, it's not so perfect.
Speed disturbs the balance,
slowness is the key.
Forgive me, my friend,
I must do this now.
Risking all I have gained, all of our love
for only the dream
that it could have been.

Chapter 27:
The Princess at the Ball—Every Relationship Is Special

When the princess who wanted to get married would go out to the ball, she would watch and wait for the person she thought was her prince holding the other slipper. She did not want to dance with anyone else who did not seem to have the slipper that would fit her other foot.

From a very early age, we are bombarded with the expectation of a special relationship. We have built our society around the world of couples. The fairy tales we watched as children were about princesses finding their princes. Somehow, it becomes our belief that we are not good enough without a significant other in our lives. There is a feeling of being left out if you don't have a partner. No one wants to be the girl at the ball who is not dancing because she does not have a partner. Are you the type who dances whenever the mood strikes? I admire the person who can dance freely with anyone or alone. I get so self-conscious when I dance that I require a partner.

It is no wonder that, at some point in our lives, we search for that special relationship—that relationship that is unique unto itself. Again, this brings me back to *A Course in Miracles*[1] and its discussion of special relationships. What I have taken from my readings is that, if I develop a special relationship with just one person, it becomes exclusive rather than inclusive. Every message that we receive about God's love is that it is inclusive and that we are all one. God's love does not exclude anyone. Yet, typically, marriage and sex are between two people. There is often a special connection between couples. When there is a true heart connection with the other person, the purpose of the ball is not to find Prince Charming, the ball is just a celebration of love. We get to choose whether our relationships are going to be about getting our ego what it wants or celebrating all that is right in this world. We dance with many different people throughout life. We dance in many different styles. Dancing is a form of celebration. Doesn't it feel good when you dance? I know I feel great when I dance—once I stop worrying about what other people might think.

A Tree

can be soft, yet firm enough

to withstand the varied seasons,

simple by all appearances, yet

complex at the roots,

able to provide, nurture, and shelter

as only a mother can (with

arms as branches that

reach out to accept, hold, comfort, and support).

Standing alone, unprotected, and vulnerable—

subject to the forces of nature.

In the grove, it is protected and safe from the storms.

A simple tree,

Ever-nourishing and providing—

the true gift of life.

I wrote this poem while thinking about a mother's love for all of her children. She will love and nurture all of her children, just like the tree that stands tall, reaches out to the sun to gather nutrients, and transfers those nutrients to the smaller saplings below. The smaller saplings will grow, even though they are unable to reach the rays.

Each of us has a special and unique gift to offer this world. I was told once that I was a gift that should be shared with the world, not shared with only one person.

What is a good man but a bad man's teacher?

What is a bad man, but a good man's job?[2]

When we give up the search or the need to find that special relationship and start to see every relationship as special and unique, there is a peace that follows. For years, the princess searched for that one special person, her prince, to share life in the castle and beyond. The princess has started to realize what it means to love everyone. When we are able to love another from the heart, there is no judgment, only compassion. You sense the other person's essence. To love another is to understand his or her pain and suffering. There might not be more that we can do for someone else besides praying for them—but at least we can do that.

There is a story by Leo Tolstoy[3] about a king in search of the answers to three questions:

1. When is the best time to do things?
2. Who is the most important one?
3. What is the right thing to do?

During his journey, he ends up saving a man who was trying to harm him. The answers to these questions have been put forward again and again by almost every author.

The answer to the first question is contained within the title of this book. The best time to do something is *now*. For me that is getting my mind out of the past and away from the future, where it seems to want to spent a great deal of time. I would say my tendency is more on the past, and thinking about what I wanted but did not get from past relationships. I also have a strong tendency to think my life would be better if I had a specific (ideal) relationship.

The answer to the second question is revealed when we focus on our special relationships with everyone. The most important one is the one you are with at the moment. When I am at work with clients, that client is the most important one. When I am with a friend, that friend is the most important one. I know that I don't always do this. For me this takes a great deal of concentrated effort. My mind likes to multitask and sometimes it feels as thought it is running at mock speed. I need to focus on taking the time to stop and listen—to really listen—to the person who I am with in the now.

The third answer is simple: do good in each moment for those who are with you. The third answer is related to purpose. Knowing your purpose (or the true purpose of the relationship from the level of the soul, not the ego) is one of my goals. Not just with one special relationship, but with any relationship.

When I wonder why something turned out the way it did— why a relationship did not work out—I think about how my situation is what it is and how it allows me to help someone in need.

The princess, as she moved forward in her life and decided that it was time to build her own castle, underwent a great deal of turmoil. Out of the turmoil came growth. In her own castle, she was able to be of service to others in their time of need. The princess did meet a prince, and he was definitely charming, but she let fear of loss, change, and uncertainty keep her chained to her current way of life. And then the universe presented her with a huge opportunity for healing and growth that she was not expecting (and that she might not have considered had she been with the same prince). Life has a way of giving you the experiences that you really, really need—whether you know it or not.

CHAPTER 28:
SELF-LOVE

You cannot love someone else more than you love yourself.

The princess first heard this from her kindred spirit and friend Brianne. She then came across it in several of her readings. Again, I love the concept that it is not about self-improvement—that implies that there is something wrong with us. It is about self-love and self-acceptance. We seek out relationships that make us feel good about ourselves and feel accepted.

If you seek out a relationship that will help you fill a void or hole in your life (an empty spot where you do not feel adequate or good enough about yourself), it is like putting the other person up on a pedestal and admitting that you see yourself as less than the other person. What happens if that other person fails to meet your expectations? If you are relying on that other person to meet your needs, you might start to build resentment towards him or her. You give that person too much power and control. How do you get your power back? You might try to knock the person off the pillar.

The person who feels less than adequate is standing in the shadow of the other person, and therefore, the first person cannot grow (unless the other person is willing to provide the nutrition to help him or her grow). Instead, you should love yourself, be okay with being alone, and be your own best friend. Having self-confidence, self-esteem, and a belief in yourself (that you are worthy of receiving all that is good and that you deserve only the best that life has to offer) makes a difference in how the relationship works. It cannot just be one person who feels that way for it to be an equal partnership. Both people must feel that way for the relationship to be unselfish and equal.

**My soul gets infused with happiness every
time I am showered by your love for me.**

It is my responsibility to keep myself happy, but there is a sense of added joy when we experience a sense of connection and belonging with others. The thoughts of separateness create suffering for us. Thoughts of connection bring us joy. But it is still our own responsibility to do this. Ghandi stated "Be the change that you want to see in the world," which I have heard from several sources. What this implies to me is that if I want to experience joy, be joy; if I want to experience love, be love; if I want to experience peace, be peace; if I want to experience connection, connect.

Part of being able to practice self-love is being able to identify areas in your life in which you are not practicing self-love. It is important to identify your own potholes or areas of deficiency. One summer, I was listening to *The Art of Extreme Self Care* by Cheryl Richardson.[1] Her discussion on deprivation really caught my attention. Growth, for me, comes not from reading or listening to what others are writing or speaking, but from doing the self-reflection work. So I did the exercises and asked myself: *Where in my life do I feel deprived?* And my answers were as follows:

1. Companionship
2. Intimacy
3. Affection
4. Connection

I thought to myself, *Oh great. All of these areas where I feel deprived require another person, which is what I don't have.* I felt worse, not better. I wanted to ask Cheryl, "Now what?" Not having an answer, I went to bed. I journaled about that topic the next morning, and I realized that I was looking at needing all of these things from the perspective of one person (because that is what I was conditioned to believe had to happen). In terms of companionship, I might not have the full attention of the person I want to have at the moment—and I may be spending evenings by myself for the first time in a long time—but I have a few close friends who I can call and chat with or see. I don't have to rely on just one person. I also shifted my thinking, and I saw an opportunity to become my own best friend. As I told my friend (who had not been as available and who was feeling badly about that), "As much as I hate being away from you—and being forced to face my own issues has sucked because I have always managed to keep myself so busy that I never had to face myself—I have been learning a lot about myself, and I think I am falling in love with me."

In terms of intimacy, this view was a challenge because I typically think of *physical* intimacy when I think about intimacy. Further examination of this involved asking myself the question, *What is it about physical intimacy that I'm missing?* The first thought was the good feelings that went along with it. For me, it was like a drug. The thing is, I am not an addict—I have proven that I can live without the physical intimacy of another for extended periods of time.

To be honest, as soon as the relationship moves to physical intimacy, I often start to fear loss. I start to find myself becoming more controlling and more jealous. This happens because what the person offers through physical intimacy fills a void in my own feelings of self-worth. Having that void filled elates me and excites me. I feel complete and desired. Therefore, now that I feel complete, I don't want to lose the feeling. If it goes away, the emptiness inside myself returns. This is the risk of filling the empty spots within yourself with something external. In order to avoid this pothole, you need to find out what it is that is missing from your self ... and then find a way to fill the hole from the inside out.

What I wanted to change was my thinking that I needed physical intimacy to feel desirable and wanted. The Louise

Hay exercises that entail looking in the mirror and saying, "I love you, Wendy Bowen" shifted my feelings on this issue. When I did this, unlike the experience Cheryl Richardson describes, I felt a surge of power. It felt better to me than having another person tell me he loved me. The next exercise for me was saying, "You are beautiful."

What I discovered when I looked at affection was that all I needed to do was shift what I saw as affection. I did this with connection as well. I have a strong connection with my mom and dad, my sister, my co-workers, my clients, and my good friends.

By shifting my thoughts in all these areas and re-examining them, I realized that I was not deprived at all. Rather, I was very blessed! Yes, perhaps I did not get all of these from one person at any given time, but they were all present in my life (okay, except for the sexual intimacy).

Giving up the need to please others is also the beginning of practicing self-love. Cheryl Richardson dedicates a whole chapter to the issue of not wanting to disappoint other people. I have already mentioned why I have a strong need to please others. This is a two-way street, and I have recognized where in my relationships I have felt disappointed.

It is difficult to hear another person tell you that he or she is going to focus on what is best for him or her (not what is going to make you happy). I do get disappointed when this happens, but it does not mean that I don't understand. I was listening to Robert Holden's Hay House radio talk show, *Shift Happens,*[2] and he stated that, "You can't get hurt in a relationship or disappointed unless you are expecting something from the relationship." This was a huge wake-up call for me. When I feel disappointed because something is not happening in a relationship that I want to happen, a great question to examine is as follows:

"What do I want from this relationship with this person?"

It does not feel good to me if I sense or find out that someone has spent time with me out of a sense of obligation rather than because it is something the person really wanted to do (because it brings about joy and happiness). Therefore, why would I think that the reverse would not be true? If someone knew that I was doing something only to please him—and that I really did not want to do it—how would that person feel?

I do hate disappointing people in my life. Not wanting to disappoint others is part of the key to my success in school, my career, and team sports. At the same time, I have not wanted to disappoint myself. There are other times in my life when I have done things I have not really wanted to do because I did not know how to deal with the feelings I had when I said no.

When we give from a place of unconditional love, we are giving without expectations. When we are expecting something from someone else, we feel disappointed when it does not happen. Disappointment is a signal that you are not giving unconditionally. At least that is what it has become for me. To give unconditionally is to provide the support for another that will empower that person, not disempower that person.

Knowing the intentions behind your giving is how you will know you are giving from a place of love (versus fear). We empower others when we give from a place of love, without expectations of love, appreciation, attention, affection, time, and a number of other things that the ego desires from another person.

CHAPTER 29:
SPIRITUAL PRACTICE

A message that I have heard consistently since starting my spiritual growth spurt is that we are spiritual beings having a human experience.

As mentioned earlier, I had a shift when I was thirty-eight years old. I was drowning in my career. I was out of balance. What was missing was the spiritual practice. I was working long hours, doing a lot of course work for my career, and fitting in physical exercise. There were days when I did a run at five o'clock in the morning. It felt very tranquil and peaceful at that time of the morning, but the purpose of the run was the physical benefits. What saved me was a shift back to my spiritual self. I started with reading books by Wayne Dyer, and then I read ones he recommended. I read daily. And then I added daily journaling. Instead of putting all my time and resources into career development, I started to attend some inspirational conferences in 2010 and 2011. I continue to read and journal daily, and I use my meditation tape when I am waking up and falling asleep. I listen to Hay House radio when puttering in my kitchen. I have purchased several CD sets so I can listen to them while driving (or sometimes while walking or doing yard work).

It is through taking the time to add these activities into my life that I have added peace to my life. Part of my routine is as follows: when I am leaving for work in the mornings, I hit shuffle on the Wayne Dyer *Change Your Thoughts, Change Your*

Life CD,[1] and I listen at random to my Tao lesson for the day. The universe gives me the message that I need to hear with regards to whatever issue might be challenging my peacefulness.

The other day, when I was really struggling with a relationship issue, I hit shuffle on Caroline Myss's *Defy Gravity.* [2] Before I hit play, I was walking and said a little prayer. I asked for the grace of fortitude (the ability to endure). What came up when I hit play was the grace of fortitude. I listened to the whole talk about fortitude, and I felt my peace return.

Having a daily spiritual practice is like pulling the weeds in your garden. The negative thoughts or self-talk grow in our minds like weeds in the garden. We pull them all one day, and new ones reappear the next day. If we don't tend to the garden for a few days—or even a week—the weeds take over. The weeds will rob the plants that you want to grow of the essential nutrients that help them grow.

Tend to your garden on a daily basis so you can grow and reach your highest and best potential.

Nurture Love

There was not beginning

nor an ending,

just the blending

of two souls,

of two bodies—

merged into one for the moment.

Two hearts pounding

in perfect harmony:

racing,

flowing

with desire and passion.

CHAPTER 30:
BE OF SERVICE

Again, the questions from *A Course in Miracles*[1] come to mind when I think about being of service:

> What would you have me do?
>
> What would you have me say?
>
> Where would you have me go?

What I have discovered is that, when my ego desires start to take precedence in my life, things get hard. I start to take everything personally. But when I go back to thinking, *How may I serve* instead of *What's in this for me?* I feel more at peace with where everything is in the moment. I think less about what my future will be. Still, I recently came to realize that I do not have to be a martyr and sacrifice my own peace and health for the sake of another person.

It is my mission to add value and make a difference in the lives of others—and to inspire people as I have been inspired. I love the prayer of St. Francis:[2]

> Lord, make me an instrument of thy peace
>
> Where there is hatred, let me sow love
>
> Where there is injury, pardon
>
> Where there is doubt, faith
>
> Where there is despair, hope

Where there is darkness, light

Where there is sadness, joy

Seek not to be understood but to understand

For it is in giving that we receive..

I know that it is my ego that wants me to believe it is a dog-eat-dog world and that I have to take care of myself first and foremost. My ego tells me I can't escape the world of competition and there always has to be a winner and a loser. Yet one of the principles of success is to adopt a win-win attitude. Can you have two winners? This idea is conveyed in the last line of the prayer of St. Francis: "For it is in giving that we receive."

Being of service is not sacrifice (as the ego would have us believe). When we help others, we really do help ourselves. This does not mean tireless hours of giving and not taking time for yourself (remember: we need our daily spiritual practice and self-love in order to be our best).

When we operate in a spirit of competition, we are excluding others and making relationships or groups exclusive. When we operate from a spirit of cooperation, we include others. We want for others what we want for ourselves. We act from love and abundance rather than fear. We can use the other person's excellence to help motivate ourselves to reach our highest and best good. We can celebrate in the success of others and learn from their success. One of my principles is, "If they can do it, so can I—as long as I want it and am willing to do what it takes."

When I operate from a place of serving rather than demanding, things tend to flow better in my life, and I feel like I am flowing gently down the stream (versus battling the rapids and trying to paddle upstream).

When the princess who wanted to get married started to look at how she was able to be of service to others, it provided a sense of purpose. Robert Holden said the following:

"Busyness is what you give your time to. A purpose is what you give your heart to."[3]

The princess took a trip to pity city to wallow in the fact that she felt alone and did not fully have the life she desired. During the trip, she took some time to do yoga. It was a way of relaxing. Her mind raced a mile a minute about all of the things that she wanted and did not have. And then a voice said to her, "It's not about you."

The princess replied, "I beg your pardon?" And the voice said it again: "It's not about you." She replied, "That's what I thought you said." There was a bit of disappointment in her voice. It was not an easy thing to hear, but in hearing it, she realized that she was expending a great deal of energy focusing on what she wanted but did not have. There was a shift that happened on that day, but the princess still needs to continue to remind herself of this fact on a daily basis. I am but one of many souls that is in search of itself; that is in search of meaning and purpose. I am but one of many souls that wants connection and belonging with the other souls, to be connected with the source as the sunbeams are connected to the sun. We all desire to be connected with the source. We are the same, and we are from the same source. As an individual sunbeam, it is our job to shine our light upon the world, but we cannot do this if we are not connected with our source of light: love. We cannot warm and light the world as an individual beam. Only by uniting and working with the other beams can we achieve our goal. When we help others shine brighter, the whole world benefits.

Chapter 31:
Happily Ever Now—a
Promise to Myself

"Consider the whole of our time when
deciding how to spend our lives."

- unknown

It was only recently that I discovered what taking a different
street meant to me. I was at The Movers and Shakers course in
San Diego, sponsored by Hay House. Here I was learning what
I needed to do to follow my vision of public speaking. God will
send you the messengers you need in your life when you are
ready to hear the message. A lovely woman asked to sit down
beside me the first evening of the conference. Her name was
Sam Lamont. She was living in Mexico, but she was from my
hometown, Peterborough, Ontario. We had lived in the same
neighborhood and attended the same high school. What Sam
taught me that weekend was that it was okay to be my self. We
discussed relationships.

Through Sam, I was introduced to Fiona Fay (from Ireland).
We spent most of the weekend together. On Saturday night,
Fiona, Sam, and I walked down to and along the water and
experienced a wonderful time talking and laughing and
sharing thoughts and ideas. On Sunday, after the workshop
was over, Sam and I went out for dinner and continued our

great conversation. We met up with Fiona later. It was out of this conversation that I discovered what taking a new road meant to me. We were talking about marriage and vows. I mentioned the ones by Neil Donald Walsh.[1] Fiona stated that the best message that she had heard was as follows:

"I promise to keep myself happy."

This caused a total shift for me. I realized that, even after all that had happened and all that my conscious mind had read and was working on believing, I was still searching for external validation of my self-worth by seeking a relationship. On the surface, I want a relationship to be about what I wrote to my good friend just prior to leaving for the San Diego trip:

> Being committed to someone—whether it be a friendship or a romantic relationship—is about being a part of something bigger than myself. It is about doubling up on the unique and precious gifts that each person has to offer, making the good twice (if not four times) as good. It means sharing the crap that each person experiences—even if it is our own. That way, no one person gets buried in the pile. The good becomes twice as good, and the not so good becomes half as bad.

> Through my experience over the past ... years, I have recognized how my fear of loss affects my relationships. How my desire for affection and attention from another comes because I don't feel from within, my own desirability and attractiveness (physically). So when it comes to me from an external source, it fills a void in my self.

> I desire connectedness and belonging because I want to be a part of the bigger picture. But I want to feel connected as me, not someone under false pretenses (which is the struggle). It

has always (in my own mind) been my athletic ability that has attracted attention and given me the in with groups (and therefore, my sense of belonging).

The thought, *I promise to keep my self happy,* has stayed with me every day since that conference. The angels brought me Sam with whom I could feel accepted for being totally me. I felt loved and accepted by this new kindred spirit in my life. It was through Sam that I met Fiona, and she brought me the message that I believe will change my life and how I look at myself and my relationships. I have become a messenger of this message.

Chapter 32:
Loving with Awareness

"Life will bring you anything you ask of it, but you have to ask."[1]

- Anthony Robins

If we are not living with awareness, we will wonder why certain events are happening to us. When we are living with awareness, we gain a sense of understanding that events are happening for us. Helping us evolve and achieve our highest and best good. I am grateful for the individuals in my life who have helped bring awareness to me and helped me grow. It has not always been easy to be aware of the part of myself that feels jealousy, separation, individualism, fear, anger, doubt, despair, and sorrow.

All of the tears that I have cried have been water for my growth. All of the crap in my life has been the fertilizer for my growth. All of the joy in my life has been the sunshine for my growth. There has been a great deal of awareness—even through the course of writing and rewriting this book. Each and every time I sat down and reviewed my journal entries or wrote, I became more aware of my feelings and more in touch with my soul, the essence of me.

My Soul

If you could feel my soul,
you'd feel the whisper
through the trees
of a warm summer night's
gentle loving breeze.

If you could hear my soul,
you'd hear the rain falling down,
landing on the treetops—
such a peaceful sound.

If you could see my soul
you'd see the sun peeking through the clouds,
casting rays of light
throughout the sky,
touching everything
that passes by.

If you could touch my soul,
you'd feel the warmth
of arms so tight—
wrapped around—
so full of love,
holding you all night.

My soul is love,
it melts with yours

from two to one.

Whenever you are near,

in my heart

and in my thoughts,

my soul is yours

to love, my dear.

Being able to love with awareness involves recognizing my own inner light and what my unique essence is. I have already gone through the archetypes that I feel are part of my unique being. Part of my unique gift is my ability to see the good in others and look beyond the behaviour that is being displayed. Part of learning to guide another involves me letting go of the idea that I know what is best for that person. I can lead through example, story, or by simply asking the right questions—rather than telling someone what I think he or she should do although I still catch myself doing this.

Chapter 33:
My Interior Castle

"If you don't go within, you go without."[1]

I have heard this quote several times, but I am sure it is on one of the Wayne Dyer audios that I frequently listen to.

Once the princess came out of hiding and opened her heart to the possibility of love again, she actually found herself alone for the first time in a very long time. She moved to a castle of her own. The castle seemed to echo in the emptiness. At first, the princess who wanted to get married would just stay away from her new castle as much as possible because of the haunting emptiness. But it was in this emptiness that she discovered a peacefulness within herself. She discovered her interior castle with the help of Caroline Myss.[2]

The purpose of this leg of her journey was to help her discover the peace of being by herself. She had to be alone in order to heal. She required the time to explore and discover all of the rooms of her new interior castle and to redecorate them as needed. It was not an easy time because she did not really know what she would discover in each room that she ventured into.

In one of the dungeons, she discovered what she wrote earlier about humility. In another dungeon, she examined her relationship to divine guidance and chaos. Via this relationship, she became able to recognize when the angels are giving her universal kicks in the butt. The princess knew that her relationship with the prince was no longer for her highest and best good, but she ignored the messages until they could not be ignored any longer. How much do you allow yourself to suffer before you listen to divine guidance? The princess knew for two years that it was time for change, but the chains of fear (fear of not finding anything better and disappointing or hurting the prince) kept her immobile. Trust and faith are the keys to unlocking these chains of fear. In the middle of the chaos, the princess would ask herself, *Am I going in the right direction?*

This was a frightening question, but only because she was afraid of not getting the answer that she wanted (and then needing to make changes to her route). It is the fear of change and the pain of leaving someone with whom you have a heart connection that kept the princess stuck in chaos. Out of the dungeon of chaos, however, has come the ability to find joy from within.

The princess had to look at who she had trapped in the darkness of her own dungeon. Through extending love to these prisoners (whom she had felt wronged and hurt by), she was able to release them. The princess would at times recapture them and imprison them again, only to go through the process of using the key of love and forgiveness to set them free again.

As the princess continued her journey into her castle, she discovered who God was to her and who she was to God.

God is the wind and the waves,

the sun and the moon,

the earth and the stars,

the trees, grass, and rocks.

God is all the animals and the living creatures.

God is beauty and grace.

God is the strength and courage within myself.

God is my love and compassion, my joy, and my laughter.

God is that part of myself that loves and accepts
everything and loves everybody without judgment.

God is my grace.

To God, I am love.

God's love feels like

the warmth of the sun on my skin,

a cool breeze on a hot day,

the sound of a child's laughter,

the waves crashing upon the shore,

the loving embrace from another,

a friendly smile from a stranger,

the warm fire and blanket on a cold night,

sand between my toes,

swimming beside the turtles in the ocean,

a beautiful sunrise or sunset,

the sound of rain.

God's love is the rainbow in the sky,

sitting silently watching the heron fish,

seeing the whales breech out in the massive ocean.

God's love is helping another feel love and joy.

Part VI:
Happily Ever Now

CHAPTER 34:
ENJOY THE JOURNEY

Regardless of the outcome, I have grown in the consciousness of love

Gratitude is the thread that sows the seeds of love that connect us all. I am very grateful for each person who has travelled with me so far on my journey. Whether the person has travelled with me for a long time (my family, for instance) or a short time, each person has contributed to my personal growth and evolution. I have felt the pains of a broken heart because I have loved. I promised myself once (after experiencing a tremendous heartbreak) that I would never let myself get hurt like that again. I locked my heart up in a cage and did not allow anyone too close to it. The relationships I had afterwards were not complete until I broke the promise to myself and let my heart out of the cage.

Though I may experience heartache in relationships, my I will keep my heart open to love. I will not let it crawl back into it's cage because I have come to realize that love—to give and receive it—is one of the most amazing and natural things in the world. It feels so wonderful, which is why, when we don't feel it or feel that we have lost it, there is pain. There is a joy in falling in love, but there is also the joy you start to feel when you fall in love with yourself. Through this journey, I have slowly recognized my patterns of subconscious programming and how they affect the relationships in my life, including the one I have with my self. My heart is staying open to receiving love—both from within myself and externally. I do not know when, how, or from where the next love-filled relationship will emerge, but my heart is staying open and on the frequency of giving and receiving love. I am ready to receive love in all of its glory. I do not have to search for it because I am developing a loving relationship with myself (my authentic self or *God being*) that will fill me from the inside out. I will fill the voids and potholes with God's love, which is the love for myself that comes from within.

It is my desire to love from a higher level of consciousness, not from desire (which can produce jealousy), not from a fear of loss (which often precedes the loss). It is my desire to love from a place of allowing, accepting, and being compassionate. All the potholes along my chosen roads are really just pointing out to me that I do not fully love at the level of unconditional love. By letting go of my desires and fears of being alone, I can elevate myself.

What I realize is that true love does not go away … nor does it fade away. The expression of it might change, though, because each person has moved forward on his or her own road.

A Day at Most

There is magic in a rainbow
as the rain drifts down.
The sunlight brightens up the sky,
although you see a frown.
There is beauty in the stars, so far—
sometimes hard to reach,
but imagination takes you there,
a special thought to each.
There is peace in the morning fog,
sometimes hard to see
where the next step takes you—

there's uncertainty.
There is grace in the eagle's flight,
soaring all alone,
searching for a place to land
among a land of stone.
There is tenderness within the sea
and power in the waves
that draw many to the shores
and others to their graves.
There is laughter in the wind
as it whistles through the land,
a gentle breeze relieves us—
destruction close at hand.
There is life among the living,
fear among the dead.
Love among the lovers,
Who share their lives instead
of never reaching outward
for fear the stars are too far—
a step that's never taken,
not knowing where they are.
There is peace within my soul—
magic, beauty, grace,
tenderness, and laughter
create a special place.
There is love in every day—
joy, pain, and sorrow—
life is but a day at most,
don't wait until tomorrow.

Thank you for allowing me to share my heart with you. I wish you all the love and happiness that life has to offer—that you deserve—as you travel on your own journey. Please remember that we spiritual beings, are just like the cells in our bodies—those cells thrive in a supportive and loving environment and join together with other cells to improve the chances of survival.

The flower grows from the rain that falls,

we grow from the tears we cry;

the flower grows from the sun that shines

we grow from the love we share.

CHAPTER 35: NEW LOVE

What would a story be without a happily ever after ending?

The princess who wanted to get married started a new love affair. She is a lovely, beautiful person. She has a gorgeous smile and smiley eyes (the kind I really like). She is tender, loving, kind, generous, caring, giving, compassionate, sensitive, and loyal. She is someone you can count on to be there if you need a friend for support. She loves animals. Although she has no children, she adores kids and gets along famously with them. She loves to laugh, and I think she has a marvelous sense of humor. She is athletic and loves nature. She is a spiritual person and loves to help others grow, evolve, and achieve their own highest potential. As a business woman, she has enjoyed much success. She enjoys travelling to new places (especially warm climates). She has a creative side—writing—and she also tries her hand at music. If you have not figured out who she is, she is me. I decided to have a love affair with myself, and I feel so very blessed and happy to have gotten to know me.

Live happily ever now!

The End

Appendix 1

My Potholes (or Pitfalls) in the Journey towards Self-Love and Self-Acceptance

1. **Fear of loss**

2. **Lack of self-worth**—It is impossible to receive the love that you desire if you do not feel worthy of it

3. **Pleasing others**—Doing things to please the other person out of a fear of disappointing that person (rather than the sense of joy you can get from giving to others)

4. **Living in the past or future**—Forgetting the now

5. **Seeking validation externally**—Looking outside of yourself for the things that you desire or feel you need

6. **Expectations placed on others**—Demanding through your actions, attention, or obligatory love and devotion (the expectation of having a relationship)

7. **Wanting what you don't have**—Looking for answers in the relationship

8. **Giving away your power**—Letting someone else drive your car and depending on that person for feeling happy, worthy, loved, and special

9. **Controlling**—Trying to control the outcome of life and others when all you really have control over are your own thoughts and actions

10. **Ego domination**

Appendix 2 :
Getting out of the
Potholes (Getting Unstuck)

1. Practice forgiveness.
2. Be flexible.
3. Allow.
4. Accept change.
5. Listen to your inner voice.
6. Love beyond the ego.
7. Outgrow your problems.
8. Take responsibility for your life.

Appendix 3:
Filling the Potholes

1. Practice self-reflection (look within).
2. Practice humility.
3. Be vulnerable.
4. Know what you really, really want.
5. See every relationship as special (grace of piety and reverence).
6. Practice self-love ("I promise to keep myself happy").

   a. Express your own wants and desires without demanding or expecting another person to fulfill them for you.

   b. Treat yourself with the same love, respect, affection, and attention that you would treat someone or something that you love.

   c. Tell yourself the things you long to hear from another. ("I love you." "You are beautiful.") Say them until you know you believe them.

7. Practice self-awareness.

   a. Honor your feelings (pay attention to how

things feel in your body and where you are feeling them) and be honest about them.

8. Be grateful daily for the abundance you do have.

9. Keep your power.

   a. Accept responsibility for your own life.

   b. Let others live their own lives.

   c. Let go of the desire for what you don't have and stop trying to get it from another person—find it within yourself (fill your own void).

10. Have faith.

    a. Just allow things to unfold—don't try to control them.

    b. Let go of the fear of loss and trust that this is a friendly universe and all will unfold according to a divine plan.

    c. Live from faith rather than fear.

11. Be of service.

FURTHER NOTES AND REFERENCES

Forward Notes
1. Quote read in *Success Intelligence, Hay House, 2008.*
2. Carolyn Myss *Entering the Castle, An Inner Path to God and Your Soul,*(New York, Free Press, 2007)

Preface
1. Carolyn Myss, *Sacred Contracts Awakening Your Divine Potential* (New York: Three Rivers Press, 2002).
2. A.A. Milne, *Winnie The Pooh,* (Dutton Children's Books, 1994).
3. Don Miguel Ruiz, *The Four Agreements* (California: Amber-Allen Publishing, 1997).

Acknowledgements
1. Heard on Wayne Dyer, *Change Your Thoughts, Change Your Life-* audio book (USA, Hay House, 2007).
2. Carolyn Myss, *Anatomy of the Spirit.* (New York, Harmony Book, 1996).

Introduction

Our Own Journey
1. Hayhouse Radio (http://www.hayhouseradio.com)

2. Fiona Fay, *Who is God? You Are,* (New York, iUniverse Inc. 2010).

3. Mary Stevenson, *Footprints poem* (http://www.footprints-inthe-sand.com/index.php?page=Poem/Poem.php)

4. Robert Holden, *I Can Do It Conference,* Vancouver BC, 2011

5. Les Brown, Keynote speaker at Univera Conference Seattle 2012

Part I Awakening

1. Wayne Dyer, *Wisdom of the Ages 60 Days to Enlightenment* (New York, HaperCollins Publishers, 1998).

Chapter 2: Discovery of the Ego

1. *A Course In Miracles,* (Foundation for Inner Peace, 2007)

2. Comment from Robert Holden, *Shift Happens talk show,* Hay House Radio (http://www.hayhouseradio.com)

3. Wayne Dyer, CD collection, *Excuses Be Gone – How to Change Life Long Defeating Thinking Habits* (USA, Hay House, 2009).

4. Jill Bolte Taylor, *My Stroke of Insight – A Brain Scientist's Personal Journey* (New York, Viking Penguin Group, 2006).

5. Wayne Dyer, *Change Your Thoughts, Change Your Life-Living the Wisdom of the Tao* (USA, Hay House Inc, 2007).

Chapter 3: The Princess at the Ball—the Need to Be Special

1. Wayne Dyer, *Change Your Thoughts, Change Your Life-Living the Wisdom of the Tao* (USA, Hay House Inc, 2007).

2. Carolyn Myss, *The Energetics of Healing – DVD collection* (Sounds True, 1997).

Chapter 4: The Desire to Be Perfect

1. Doreen Virtue, PH.D., Healing With The Angles, Oracle Cards, (California, Hay House, 1999).

2. Wayne Dyer, *Change Your Thoughts, Change Your Life- Living the Wisdom of the Tao* (USA, Hay House Inc, 2007).

3. Robert Holden, *Shift Happens Radio show*, Hayhouse Radio (http://www.hayhouseradio.com)

Chapter Five: The Fear of Loss and Being Alone

1. Rhonda Byrne, *The Secret* CD audio collection (Simon & Schuster Audio/Beyond Words, 2006).

2. Heard on Wayne Dyer, *Change Your Thoughts, Change Your Life-* audio book (USA, Hay House, 2007).

Chapter 6: Know Thyself

1. Carolyn Myss, *Sacred Contracts Awakening Your Divine Potential* (New York: Three Rivers Press, 2002).

2. Eckart Tolle, *A New Earth Awakening to Your Life's Purpose*, (New York, Plume, 2005).

3. Robert Holden, *Shift Happens*, (California, Hay House Inc. 2000).

4. Bruce Lipton, *Biology of Belief – Unleashing the Power of Consciousness, Matter, and Miracles* (USA, Hay House, 2008).

5. *Secrets of a Millionaire Mind- Mastering the Inner Game of Wealth* (New York, HaperCollins Books, 2005).

6. Depak Chopra, *Buddha – A Story of Enlightenment* (USA, HarperCollins, 2007).

7. Robert Holden, *Shift Happens*, (California, Hay House Inc. 2000)

8. Carolyn Myss, *Entering the Castle, An Inner Path to God and Your Soul*, (New York, Free Press, 2007).

Chapter 7: Giving Away Your Power

1. Wayne Dyer, *Change Your Thoughts, Change Your Life-Living the Wisdom of the Tao* (USA, Hay House Inc, 2007).

2. Carolyn Myss, *The Energetics of Healing – DVD collection* (Sounds True, 1997).

3. Doreen Virtue, PH.D., Healing With The Angles, Oracle Cards, (California, Hay House, 1999).

4. Carol McCloud, *Have You Filled Your Bucket Today? A Guide to Daily Happiness for Kids,* (Ferne Press, Northville MI, 2006).

Chapter 8: Living without Regrets

1. Reference to the Monsters Inc. Movie, 2001; written by Pete Docter, A Walt Disney Production.

2. Wayne Dyer, CD collection, *Excuses Be Gone – How to Change Life Long Defeating Thinking Habits* (USA, Hay House, 2009).

3. Richard Brodie, *Viruses of the Mind* (Integral Press, 2004).

4. Alvyn M Freed, *TA for Tots and Other Pinzes* (Jalmar Press, 1973).

5. Robert Holden, *Shift Happens,* (California, Hay House Inc. 2000)

6. In a facebook conversation with Clemens Rettich, Business Coach (http://clemensrettich.com)

7. Robert Holden, *I Can Do It Conference, Vancouver* BC, 2011

Chapter 9: The End of the Fairy Tale

1. Bruce Lipton, *Biology of Belief – Unleashing the Power of Consciousness, Matter, and Miracles* (USA, Hay House, 2008).

2. Tim Burton movie, Alice In Wonderland; Walt Disney Productions 2010.

Chapter 10: The Princess Tries to Rescue Herself—Independence

1. Wayne Dyer, CD collection, *Excuses Be Gone – How to Change Life Long Defeating Thinking Habits* (USA, Hay House, 2009).

2. Robert Holden, *Shift Happens*, (California, Hay House Inc. 2000).

Chapter 11: Prince Charming—Feeling Loved and Safe

1. Wayne Dyer, CD collection, *Excuses Be Gone – How to Change Life Long Defeating Thinking Habits* (USA, Hay House, 2009).

2. Fiona Fay, *Who is God? You Are,* (New York, iUniverse Inc. 2010).

3. Neil Donald Walsh, *Conversations With God,* (New York, Hampton Roads, 2005).

4. Wayne Dyer, *Inspiration Your Ultimate Calling* audio (USA, Hay House, 2006).

Chapter 12: Surviving Turmoil and Change

1. Don Miguel Ruiz, *The Four Agreements* (California: Amber-Allen Publishing, 1997).

2. John Harricharan, *When You Can Walk on Water, Take the Boat,* (New World Publishing, 1988).

3. Heard on Wayne Dyer, *Change Your Thoughts, Change Your Life-* audio book (USA, Hay House, 2007).

4. Robert Holden, *Shift Happens Radio show,* Hayhouse Radio (http://www.hayhouseradio.com)

5. Robert Anthony, *The Ultimate Secrets of Total Self-Confidence* (San Diego, CA, New Thoughts Publications, 1979).

6. Don Miguel Ruiz, *The Fifth Agreement* (California: Amber-Allen Publishing, 2010).

7. Neil Donald Walsh, *When Everything Changes, Change Everything*, (Ashland, OR, EmNin Books, 2009).

8. Elizabeth Kubler Ross, Heard on an online Oprah Podcast discussion

Chapter 13: Validating Love—the Doghouse Theory

Chapter 14: Constant Transformation

1. Karl Paul Reinhold Niebuhr *Serenity Prayer*

2. Robert Anthony, *The Ultimate Secrets of Total Self-Confidence* (San Diego, CA, New Thoughts Publications, 1979).

3. Miyamoto Musashi (Translated by Thomas Cleary) *,Book of Five Rings* (USA, Random House, 1993).

Part II: Climbing out of the Potholes

Chapter 15: Forgiveness Is the Key

1. Heard on Wayne Dyer, *Change Your Thoughts, Change Your Life-* audio book (USA, Hay House, 2007).

2. Robin Sharma's, *The Monk Who Sold His Ferrari* (New York, HarperCollins, 2007).

3. *A Course In Miracles,* (Foundation for Inner Peace, 2007)

Chapter 16: Being Flexible

1. Heard on Wayne Dyer, *Change Your Thoughts, Change Your Life-* audio book (USA, Hay House, 2007).

2. Neil Donald Walsh, *When Everything Changes, Change Everything*, (Ashland, OR, EmNin Books, 2009).

Chapter 17: Allowing

1. Heard on Caroline Myss, *Defy Gravity – Healing Beyond the Bounds of Reason* - audio (USA, Hay House 2009).

2. Heard on Wayne Dyer, *Change Your Thoughts, Change Your Life*- audio book (USA, Hay House, 2007).

3. Louise Hay, *You Can Heal Your Life* (USA, Hay House, 2004).

4. Deepak Chopra, *Reinventing the Body, Resurrecting the Soul* (New York, Harmony Books, 2009)

Chapter 18: The Universal Kick in the Butt—Accepting Change

1. Neil Donald Walsh, *When Everything Changes, Change Everything*, (Ashland, OR, EmNin Books, 2009).

Chapter 19: Your Inner Voice— Finding It and Listening to It

1. Carolyn Myss, *The Energetics of Healing – DVD collection* (Sounds True, 1997).

2. LOUISE L. HAY, MICHAEL GOORJIAN, *Painting the Future, Tales of Everyday Magic*, (Hay House, May 2012)

3. Heard on Wayne Dyer, *Change Your Thoughts, Change Your Life*- audio book (USA, Hay House, 2007).

4. Eckart Tolle, *A New Earth Awakening to Your Life's Purpose*, (New York, Plume, 2005).

Chapter 20: Loving Beyond the Ego

1. *A Course In Miracles*, (Foundation for Inner Peace, 2007)

2. Heard on Wayne Dyer, *Change Your Thoughts, Change Your Life*- audio book (USA, Hay House, 2007).

3. Neil Donald Walsh, *Conversations With God*, (New York, Hampton Roads, 2005).

Chapter 21: Outgrow Your Problem

1. Heard on Wayne Dyer, *Change Your Thoughts, Change Your Life*- audio book (USA, Hay House, 2007).

2. Robert Holden, *Shift Happens Radio show,* Hayhouse Radio (http://www.hayhouseradio.com)

Chapter 22: Escaping from the Dungeon— Take Responsibility for Your Life

1. Carolyn Myss, *The Energetics of Healing – DVD collection* (Sounds True, 1997).

2. Heard on Wayne Dyer, *Change Your Thoughts, Change Your Life-* audio book (USA, Hay House, 2007).

3. Neil Donald Walsh, *Conversations With God,* (New York, Hampton Roads, 2005).

4. Marlo Mogan, *Mutant Messages Down Under* (New York, HarperCollins, 1994).

Part III: Avoid the Potholes—Take a Different Road

Chapter 23: Mirror, Mirror

Chapter 24: Humility

1. Heard on Wayne Dyer, *Change Your Thoughts, Change Your Life-* audio book (USA, Hay House, 2007).

Chapter 25: Vulnerability

Chapter 26: Knowing What You Really Want

1. Heard on Robert Holden's *Success Intelligence* – audio book (USA, Hay House, 2008).

2. Carolyn Myss, *Entering the Castle, An Inner Path to God and Your Soul,* (New York, Free Press, 2007).

Chapter 27: The Princess at the Ball— Every Relationship Is Special

1. *A Course In Miracles,* (Foundation for Inner Peace, 2007)

2. Heard on Wayne Dyer, *Change Your Thoughts, Change Your Life-* audio book (USA, Hay House, 2007).

3. Leo Tolstoy, The Three Questions.

Chapter 28: Self-Love

1. Heard on Cheryl Richardson *The Art of Extreme Self Care* – audio book (USA, Hay House, 2009).

2. Robert Holden, *Shift Happens Radio show,* Hay House Radio (http://www.hayhouseradio.com)

Chapter 29: Spiritual Practice

1. Heard on Wayne Dyer, *Change Your Thoughts, Change Your Life-* audio book (USA, Hay House, 2007).

2. Caroline Myss, *Defy Gravity – Healing Beyond the Bounds of Reason -* audio (USA, Hay House 2009).

Chapter 30: Be of Service

1. *A Course In Miracles,* (Foundation for Inner Peace, 2007)

2. *Prayer of St. Francis* (found on internet Wikipedia)

3. Heard on Robert Holden's *Success Intelligence* – audio book (USA, Hay House, 2008).

Chapter 31: Happily Ever Now—a Promise to Myself

1. Neil Donald Walsh, *Conversations With God,* (New York, Hampton Roads, 2005).

Chapter 32: Loving with Awareness

1. Anthony Robins, *Unlimited Power* (New York, Free Press, 1986).

Chapter 33: My Interior Castle

1. Wayne Dyer, CD collection, *Excuses Be Gone – How to Change Life Long Defeating Thinking Habits* (USA, Hay House, 2009).

2. Carolyn Myss, *Entering the Castle, An Inner Path to God and Your Soul,* (New York, Free Press, 2007).

Part VI: Happily Ever Now

Chapter 34: Enjoy the Journey

Chapter 35: New Love

CPSIA information can be obtained at www.ICGtesting.com
Printed in the USA
LVOW060711040413

327469LV00002B/2/P